GAME CHANGERS

The Greatest Plays in
Penn State
Football History

Lou Prato

TRIUMPH
B O O K S

This book is dedicated to the hundreds of Penn State football players since 1887 who made the game-changing plays that helped the Nittany Lions become one of the great teams in college football

Triumph Books and colophon are registered trademarks of Random House, Inc.

Library of Congress Cataloging-in-Publication Data

Prato, Lou.
  Game changers : the greatest plays in Penn State football history / Lou Prato.
    p. cm.
  Includes bibliographical references.
  ISBN-13: 978-1-60078-259-6
  ISBN-10: 1-60078-259-0
  1. Penn State Nittany Lions (Football team)—History. 2. Pennsylvania State University—Football—History. I. Title.
  GV958.P46P72 2009082
  796.332'630974853—dc22

                                                                          2009025249

This book is available in quantity at special discounts for your group or organization. For further information, contact:
  Triumph Books
  542 South Dearborn Street
  Suite 750
  Chicago, Illinois 60605
  (312) 939-3330
  Fax (312) 663-3557
  www.triumphbooks.com

Printed in China
ISBN: 978-1-60078-259-6
Design by Sue Knopf/Patricia Frey
Page production by Patricia Frey

Contents

Foreword

Joe Paterno used to tell us that big games nearly always come down to a handful of plays that determine the outcome. They can happen on offense, defense, or in the kicking game, and you never know exactly when during the course of the contest these game-changing plays will occur. I had the great privilege of being the starting quarterback at Penn State for 32 games from 1980 to 1982. I was involved in more than 2,000 offensive plays during my collegiate career, but a special few have left an indelible mark on my life and memories.

Two plays particularly stand out for me during our national championship season of 1982, and they are detailed in the pages of this book by Lou Prato. I will never forget our third-string tight end Kirk Bowman cradling a low (and not very well-thrown) pass in the back of the end zone with four seconds remaining to beat highly ranked Nebraska in the first night game ever played at Beaver Stadium. The play culminated in a game-winning drive that started on our own 35-yard line with a little over a minute to play in the game. (Here is an interesting footnote: for the entire season, Kirk Bowman had two receptions; both were against Nebraska, both were on the same play-call, and both went for touchdowns!)

The other play that remains fresh in my memory occurred in the 1983 Sugar Bowl. While leading top-ranked Georgia 20–17 in the fourth quarter, seven consecutive running plays had moved us across midfield, setting up my most memorable play as a Nittany Lion. We called a play-action pass, and Gregg Garrity ran by a freshman cornerback, Tony Flack, to make a diving catch in the end zone for a 47-yard touchdown that put us up by 10. The Bulldogs would score once more, but Gregg's catch provided the cushion we needed to secure Penn State's first national championship.

I was a little surprised when Lou Prato told me that my pass to Gregg in the Sugar Bowl was the all-time No. 1 play in this book, *Game Changers: The Greatest Plays in Penn State Football History*. I am quite honored but also humbled. Going back to the start of the Joe Paterno era at Penn State, I know there have been hundreds of Nittany Lions players—including many of my teammates—who have made great plays in all facets of the game that led to victories and helped make Penn State one of the premier football programs in the country. I am pleased to represent all the players who have worn the Blue and White down through the decades.

If you love the Nittany Lions, you will love this book. It is filled with the facts and anecdotes that tell the story of Penn State football through the years. Great plays. Great players. Key victories. Magical memories. We are…Penn State!

—Todd Blackledge

Todd Blackledge (left) poses with Penn State's athletics director, Tim Curley, after accepting the prestigious NCAA Silver Anniversary Award on January 13, 2008.

Acknowledgments

An author may write a book, but there are many others who help make it happen.

This is my fifth book, and my wife Carole has always been there with me, supporting and encouraging me all the way. She also is the first person who reads my manuscripts, picking up on my errors and offering suggestions to make my final product better.

Carole was especially dedicated and indulgent as I was writing this book. The deadline pressure was enormous, and I spent weeks on end holed up in my home office from early morning until late at night working on this project. She made a lot of sacrifices during this intense period, as I virtually became a hermit for three months. Perhaps she was most understanding when our 50th wedding anniversary occurred in the middle of it all and we spent a quiet weekend celebrating with our children and grandchildren rather than taking that trip to Italy I have been promising her. Without her continued love and help I couldn't do what I enjoy, and that's write articles and books like this one.

I am also grateful to a lot of members of the Penn State family who have continued to help me over the years. No one was more helpful with this book than Fran Fisher, the retired broadcaster and athletics department executive who is still as popular with the Penn State football nation as he was during his heyday on the air. He described most of these greatest plays to his radio audience as they were happening, and I leaned on him for research, background, and advice.

Fran also helped me compile my preliminary list of the games that had so many great plays. So did Fran's broadcast successor, Steve Jones, and my fraternity brother Ron Falk. Steve is a walking encyclopedia of the Joe Paterno coaching era and remembers details I have long ago forgotten. Ron, my friend of more than 50 years, is a one-time publishing executive and a die-hard Penn State fan who has helped me in the past with my articles and books about the Nittany Lions, and he continues to do so.

Once again, Jackie Esposito, Paul Dyzak, and Paul Karwacki at the Penn State Pattee-Paterno Library Sports Archives made their files available for my research and helped me obtain many of the historical photographs in this book. Jeff Nelson, the assistant athletics director for communications, and his gracious staff also were there again to provide any assistance I needed.

A special thanks to the photographers whose photos are a vital part of this book. Most of the photos came from the files of the Pattee-Paterno Library Sports Archives or Penn State's Athletic Communications Office. The names of the photographers responsible for those photos have been lost over the years, and that's a shame, because photographers rarely get the credit they justly deserve. But I also was able to obtain photos from the files of *Blue White Illustrated*, and I thank publisher Phil Grosz and cameramen Harvey Levine and Mark Selders. Thanks also to freelance photographers Steve Manuel and the family of the late Joe Bodkin for the photos they provided. Steve's photos have appeared in all four of my Penn State football books, including three with his photos on the cover. No one has been more helpful to me over the years than Steve.

Todd Blackledge was an obvious choice to write the foreword for this book because he was involved in so many great plays in his years as the Nittany Lions' quarterback. He epitomizes the scholar-athletes of the Paterno era—a Phi Beta Kappa and winner of the Davey O'Brien Award as the nation's best quarterback in 1982. Todd is a big-time sportscaster now, one of the best broadcasters in college football, but he never has forgotten where he started. He was surprised when I told him my No. 1 greatest play in Penn State's history was his touchdown pass to Gregg Garrity in the 1982 national championship game. Todd is also a nice guy, and I appreciate and thank him for writing the foreword.

I also want to thank Tom Bast, the editorial director of Triumph Books, for giving me another opportunity to write a book for his company. If not for Tom, I would not be having so much fun in my "senior" years. Tom has become a friend, and I look forward to visiting with him again in the future, perhaps at another spring-training baseball game in Florida.

I would be remiss if I didn't acknowledge the help of others at Triumph, especially Adam Motin and Laine Morreau, my editors. Adam provided the encouragement and advice I needed to get through those many long days in my isolated home office. And Laine was there for the details and the changes that were necessary to create the finished product. Thanks, too, to all the people at Triumph who have helped in the design, production, marketing, and sales of this book. It takes a winning team to produce a successful book, and president Mitch Rogatz has one at Triumph.

I also want to thank all the newspaper and magazine writers and the book authors who have written about Penn State football through the years. There are far too many of them to mention, even in the selected bibliography at the end of this book. Their work provided the basic information for each chapter, and for that I am extremely grateful.

However, as I have done in all my previous Penn State football books, I must single out the late Ridge Riley. Ridge was the longtime university administrator who, 70 years ago, created the weekly *Football Letter* that continues to be distributed to alumni during the season, and he was the author of the definitive history of Penn State football from 1887 to 1975, *The Road to Number One*. Every time I use those newsletters and his book in my research I learn something new. God bless you, Ridge. You will always be Penn State's No. 1 fan.

Finally, I want to thank all the hundreds of Penn State football players, coaches, and staff members since 1887 that really made this book possible. Without them, there would not be *Game Changers: The Greatest Plays in Penn State Football History*.

—Lou Prato
May 2009

Introduction

Selecting the plays for *Game Changers: The Greatest Plays in Penn State Football History* is analogous to choosing and rating the most memorable days in your married life. You and your spouse might agree on the first one or two, and maybe even a couple more, but after that you'll be fortunate if a big argument doesn't ensue. As the old saying goes, everything is in the eye of the beholder.

So, from the start it was important that criteria be established for my choices. Initially, the idea was to select 50 plays from the beginning of Penn State football in 1887 and to rank them from 1 to 50. But in an effort to produce a book that would be more familiar to today's Nittany Lions fans, the format was altered.

The revised concept was based on plays that changed the outcome of games in what is best described as "modern-day football." It also was decided to reduce the number of plays from the original 50 to 35 to give more significance to the plays selected.

With the revisions and new guidelines, I believed it would be best to concentrate on the Joe Paterno coaching era. That went back to 1950, when Paterno joined coach Rip Engle's staff, because from his first year Joe Paterno would become the preeminent individual in the rise of Penn State to become one the elite teams in the country.

My selection of plays from that period is based on how meaningful or consequential the plays were in winning that particular game as well as the impact those plays may have had on that season and in the evolution of the Penn State football program. It's also the same rationale that caused me to include just one losing game in this book. That was the 20–18 loss to Syracuse in 1959 before the largest crowd in Beaver Field history, when a couple of missed extra points may have cost the Nittany Lions the national championship.

Notice that this book's title does not contain the word *memorable*. There are a lot of memorable plays that could not meet my criteria. One such play that came quickly to mind was in the Alabama game of 1982, when blocking back Mike Suter backed into the punter at a crucial point in the fourth quarter and the Lions' defeat almost cost them the national championship. Certainly Alabama's goal-line stand in the 1978 national championship game was memorable in the most depressing and frustrating way, as was the last-minute Hail Mary pass and field goal by Minnesota that ruined the Lions' 1999 season. And anyone who saw the Illinois game in 1998 will always remember LaVar Arrington's leaping tackle to nail the ball carrier the instant he touched the ball, but the play had absolutely no bearing on winning the game.

As I continued my selection process, two more factors came into making my choices. In some games there was not only one play that was crucial and consequential but two and even three plays or more during the game. Sometimes the plays were in a two-play sequence, such as Michael Robinson's last-minute passes to Isaac Smolko and Derrick Williams in the come-from-behind win over Northwestern in 2005 and the goal-line stands against Notre Dame in 1986 and Indiana in 2004. In other games, the plays may have occurred at separate points, like the fourth-quarter interceptions by linebackers Shane Conlan and Pete Giftopoulos in the 1986 national championship game against Miami. Rather than split great plays like these into separate chapters, I combined them into one, enabling me to get more of those greatest plays into this book.

As I proceeded with the project, I eventually identified more than 100 games or plays that were possible candidates for my final *Game Changers* of the Paterno era. Weeding through the plays in a chronological order, I found some that were obvious keepers and others that were easily eliminated. But selecting the final 35 was a process steeped in tougher choices.

In my research, I sometimes found that the details of the plays were not exactly how I remembered them, and I saw many of these plays in person, dating back to 1955—the classic duel between two of the greatest players in college football, Penn State's Lenny Moore and Syracuse's Jim Brown. I combed through newspapers, magazines, books, official game films, and home-recorded videos to describe the game and the plays as accurately as possible.

There were several plays that I regret didn't make my final cut. The biggest one was the tackle by Pete Curkendall on a two-point-conversion attempt on the last play of the 1987 game against Notre Dame at Beaver Stadium that beat the No. 7 Irish 21–20. It was not only a great game but one of the coldest, most bone-chilling games I ever witnessed.

At the conclusion of the book, the reader will find a list of another 15 great plays from 1950–2008 that fit the criteria but for one reason or another didn't make the final cut. This list also includes 10 great plays from the pre-Paterno era of 1887–1949, which was also significant in the evolution of Penn State football. I know many more plays could have been included on this short list, and readers can make their own choices. But in the end, the great plays in this book were *Game Changers*, and they all helped make the Penn State football program one of the finest in the history of college football.

And that's why…

WE ARE…

PENN STATE!

Spectacular
Catches
and
Drives

January 1, 1983

The Catch

Gregg Garrity's Diving Pass Reception Wins National Championship

Gregg Garrity is not as well known as the quarterback who threw the ball to him in the 1982 national championship game at the Sugar Bowl, but it's a photograph of Garrity and not Todd Blackledge that graces the cover of *Sports Illustrated* and occupies a prominent spot in the homes of thousands of Penn State fans around the world.

Garrity's leaping dive into the end zone to grab the 47-yard pass from Blackledge early in the fourth quarter is known forever in Penn State history simply as "the Catch." It's the play that propelled the Nittany Lions to their first national championship after a long, steep, and frustrating trek to the pinnacle of college football.

Penn State had come close in 1978 when it lost the championship game to Alabama in the same Superdome, and despite three undefeated teams since 1968, it had been snubbed by the polls. This time State won it on the field New Year's night in a 27–23 win over Georgia, and the Nittany Lion nation will always remember the play that did it.

Yet, if not for some luck near the end of the regular season, the 1982 team would not have played No. 1 Georgia. Paterno believed his 1981 Lions should have played for the championship, but they had stumbled twice at Beaver Stadium in games they should have won. With the departure of 11 starters and other personnel questions on both offense and defense, it seemed unlikely that the '82 team could duplicate the 10–2 1981 season.

But with a more up-tempo passing attack and an opportunistic defense, the Lions climbed from No. 9 in the AP preseason rankings to No. 3 after a thrilling, last-second upset win over Nebraska in Game 4. However, when they lost at Alabama the next week, their championship aspirations seemed dim.

Penn State was idle on the day bowl arrangements were made because the Pitt game had been shifted to Thanksgiving. The Lions were now No. 3 again, but No. 2 SMU and No. 1 Georgia were expected to be matched up in the Sugar Bowl for the title. When Arkansas tied SMU that Saturday, State was invited instead.

The game pitted the Lions' explosive offense and attacking defense against a power-running offense featuring Heisman Trophy winner Herschel Walker and a ball-hawking defense that led the nation in interceptions.

Gregg Garrity celebrates in the end zone after making the play of the game with his diving touchdown catch in the national championship game against Georgia. *Photo courtesy of the Penn State All-Sports Museum*

Penn State's offense squares off against the Georgia defense in the 1983 Sugar Bowl. *Photo courtesy of Penn State Athletic Communications*

Because of Georgia's suspect passing game, Penn State was favored by three to four points.

The Lions grabbed control of the game after the opening kickoff with some quick-strike passes that took them 80 yards in seven plays for a touchdown, and the offense continued to be the aggressor throughout the first half as the defense kept Walker in check. With 44 seconds left in the half, Nick Gancitano's 45-yard field goal gave Penn State a 20–3 lead. But after Walker ran back the kickoff to Georgia's 34-yard line, the Bulldogs quickly passed their way downfield to make it 20–10 at halftime.

With their newfound confidence, Georgia took the second-half kickoff and again passed its way 69 yards to narrow the score to 20–17. The two defenses then took charge. The Bulldogs harassed Blackledge on blitzes while the Lions not only continued to stymie Walker but also disrupted Georgia's rejuvenated passing game with interceptions.

As the third quarter was ending, State gained possession at its own 19-yard line, and on the third play tailback Curt Warner ran up the middle for 11 yards. Three plays later the Lions had a first-and-10 at the Bulldogs' 47-yard line less than two minutes into the fourth quarter, when Paterno sent in the play 6-4-3. They had run a variation of the play out of the I-formation several times earlier, including on Warner's 11-yard run, only this time Blackledge would fake to Warner and pass to one of four receivers going deep.

Georgia bit on the fake, and Blackledge spotted Garrity way downfield on the left sideline getting a step on the Bulldogs' freshman cornerback. "I threw the ball as far as I could," Blackledge said later. Garrity saw the ball coming

The Other Catch

Gregg Garrity's best memory of the 1983 Sugar Bowl is a dinky six-yard catch he made about 13 minutes after the Catch. "It was for a first down and kept the drive going, and we could run the clock," Garrity recalled years later. "This was just as important as the catch in the end zone."

Penn State was leading Georgia 27–23 with 1:37 left in the game and a third-and-3 at the State 32. The safe play would have been a run and, if unsuccessful, a punt on fourth down. But giving the ball back to Georgia was a risk, particularly with the explosive and dangerous Herschel Walker capable of winning the game on one play. Paterno and his assistant coaches were leaning toward a conservative run up the middle. Blackledge wanted to pass. Paterno knew an interception could be catastrophic, but, as he wrote, "My gut believed in him because he was afire with belief in himself." Paterno told Blackledge, "Make sure you throw it far enough."

Georgia was completely surprised by the six-yard square-out pass to Garrity at the left sideline. "It was the last catch I ever caught at Penn State," Garrity recalled.

But hardly anyone who was in the Superdome that night or watched the game on television remembers it. Garrity calls it "the Other Catch."

and stretched as far as possible, taking the ball on his fingertips and pulling it into his chest as he slammed onto the artificial turf of the end zone. He stood up with both arms raised above his head with the ball in his right hand as photographers snapped their cameras. Gregg Garrity had just made the biggest reception in Penn State history.

There was still 13:16 left, and it would take a great defensive effort and another Blackledge pass to Garrity to finally seal the game. When the game was over, the Penn State fans stood and chanted, "We're No. 1, we're No. 1!" as the players carried Paterno off the field. No. 1 at last, thanks to the Catch.

> **S**omeone, hopefully, will be open on the play. It's four receivers against two or three defensive backs. [Blackledge] threw it well. I just hoped I could get to it. We knew they didn't have great speed in the secondary, so we were trying to take advantage of that.
>
> —GREGG GARRITY

Game Details

Penn State 27 • Georgia 23

Penn State	7	13	0	7	**27**
Georgia	3	7	7	6	**23**

Date: January 1, 1983

Team Records: Penn State 10–1, Georgia 11–0

Scoring Plays:

PSU—Warner two-yard run (Gancitano PAT)

GEO—Butler 27-yard FG

PSU—Gancitano 38-yard FG

PSU—Warner nine-yard run (Gancitano PAT)

PSU—Gancitano 45-yard FG

GEO—Archie 10-yard pass from Lastinger (Butler PAT)

GEO—Walker one-yard run (Butler PAT)

PSU—Garrity 47-yard pass from Blackledge (Gancitano PAT)

GEO—Kay nine-yard pass from Lastinger (run failed)

November 12, 1994

The Drive

Nittany Lions Drive 96 Yards in Rain Late in Fourth Quarter to Win First Big Ten Title

Never in Penn State's history has there been a late-fourth-quarter drive to win a game like the one at Illinois in 1994. Penn State has won many games since 1887 under pressure in the last minute or so, but the dynamic 14-play, 96-yard drive in the cold and dreary rain under artificial lighting inside the Illini's hostile Memorial Stadium surpassed them all.

Not only was the outcome of the game extremely significant, but there were many intriguing, adverse, and intertwined circumstances before, during, and after the game. This was Penn State's second year in the Big Ten and a month before it became No. 1 in the polls after winning at Michigan.

Yet two weeks later, when the Lions clobbered No. 16 Ohio State 63–14, they inexplicably dropped to No. 2 in the AP poll. Then, after the reserves gave up 17 points in the last six minutes at Indiana, they also fell to No. 2 in the coaches' rankings. Nebraska had become the darling of the pollsters, and that would eventually ruin the team's chances for the national championship.

When the Lions flew into Champaign, they knew they could win the Big Ten title and a trip to the Rose Bowl by beating the No. 25 Illini, but they also wanted to try and impress the poll voters.

Illinois was a 12-point underdog, but with a fired-up defense led by three outstanding linebackers, it shocked the Lions and everyone else watching in the national television audience by taking a commanding 21–0 lead 10:06 into the opening quarter. An interception, fumble recovery, and a punt deep in Lions territory led to the three quick touchdowns, and the Penn State team that had outscored its opponents 113–0 in the first quarter was in major trouble.

In the early moments of the second quarter, Illinois had the Lions backed up at their own 1-yard line and another score here by a defensive turnover or another forced punt might have made it too much for Penn State to overcome. But this is where the biggest comeback in the Joe Paterno coaching era began.

The Lions went 99 yards in 11 plays for a touchdown and minutes later scored again after a partially blocked punt set up a first-down 38-yard touchdown pass with 3:35 left in the half. But Illinois answered with another quick touchdown drive to end the first half at 28–14.

Brian Milne bursts through for the game-winning touchdown against Illinois on November 12, 1994.
Photo courtesy of Penn State Athletic Communications

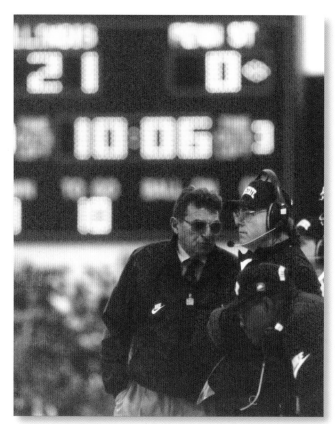

Joe Paterno stands on the sideline at the Illinois game. In the background the scoreboard reflects Penn State's 21–0 first-quarter deficit. *Photo courtesy of Steve Manuel*

Game Details

Penn State 35 • Illinois 31

Penn State	0	14	7	14	**35**
Illinois	21	7	3	0	**31**

Date: November 12, 1994

Team Records: Penn State 8–0, Illinois 6–3

Scoring Plays:

ILL—Douthard one-yard run (Richardson PAT)

ILL—Dilger one-yard pass from Johnson (Richardson PAT)

ILL—Fisher 12-yard pass from Johnson (Richardson PAT)

PSU—Milne one-yard run (Conway PAT)

PSU—Scott 38-yard pass from Collins (Conway PAT)

ILL—Douthard five-yard run (Richardson PAT)

PSU—Carter four-yard run (Conway PAT)

ILL—Richardson 37-yard FG

PSU—Milne five-yard run (Conway PAT)

PSU—Milne two-yard run (Conway PAT)

Illinois had momentum as it took the second-half kickoff, but the Lions again forced a punt to midfield, and in six plays it was a seven-point game again. However, the Illini stretched it to 10 points on a time-consuming 71-yard drive that ended with a field goal. The Lions missed a 33-yard field goal late in the third quarter, but with a light rain falling, State narrowed the lead to three points midway through the fourth period on an eight-play, 55-yard drive keyed by a 17-yard pass from quarterback Kerry Collins to Bobby Ingram on a fourth-and-2 at the Illini 41.

State's defense held again at the Illinois 29, but the Illini's booming punt over the returner's head was downed at the State 4. There was 6:07 left in the game as the rain continued and the wind picked up. "Ninety-six yards,

fellas," Collins said as he stepped into the huddle. "Let's go. Let's do it." Collins had three timeouts, but he knew he could not afford one mistake, and "the Drive" began.

In four plays and a face-mask penalty, the Lions were at their 44 with 4:25 left. Five plays later the Illini thought they had stopped State at the Illinois 35 on third-and-1, but a measurement gave State a first down with 2:26 remaining. Two more pass completions—sandwiched between a timeout—and a nine-yard run by fullback Brian Milne put the ball on the 2, and Illinois called timeout with 1:11 left

The 14 Plays of the Winning Drive

Time Clock—6:07—First-and-10 at Penn State 4-Yard Line—PS with Three Timeouts Remaining

First-and-10 at PS 4—Tailback Ki-Jana Carter runs between right tackle and right end for one yard.

Second-and-9 at PS 5—Kerry Collins throws pass near right sideline to fullback Brian Milne for six yards.

Third-and-3 at PS 11—Collins passes to tight end Kyle Brady at left hash mark off play fake for seven yards.

First-and-10 at PS 18—Collins throws to Bobby Engram near left sideline near PS bench for 11, and Illinois is penalized 15 yards for face-mask penalty to PS 44 with 4:25 on the clock.

First-and-10 at PS 44—Collins passes over middle to Carter for five yards.

Second-and-5 at PS 49—Carter sweeps left end for seven yards and goes out of bounds with 3:42 on the clock.

First-and-10 at IL 44—Milne runs up the middle for three yards.

Second-and-7 at IL 41—Collins passes to Brady on left sideline for six yards.

Third-and-1 at IL 35—Carter sweeps left end for three yards as measurement gives PS ball by half the length of the football with 2:17 on the clock.

First-and-10 at IL 34—Collins passes to Freddie Scott on slant over middle toward left sideline for 16 yards.

First-and-10 at IL 18—Carter runs up the middle for no gain and PS calls timeout with 1:43 on the clock.

Second-and-10 at IL 18—Collins passes to Engram over the middle near left hash mark for nine yards with 1:11 on the clock.

Third-and-1 at IL 9—Milne runs up middle on trap play for seven yards, and IL calls timeout with 1:00 on the clock.

First-and-Goal at the Illinois 3-Yard Line—Backup tight end Keith Olsommer and backup fullback Jason Sload enter the game.

—Offense lines up in full-house backfield formation with tight seven-man line.

—Collins hands off to Milne.

—Right side of line—guard Marco Rivera, tackle Andre Johnson, and Olsommer open running hole between right tackle and end.

—Left guard Jeff Hartings pulls as Sload and Carter shield off the outside with blocks, and Hartings leads Milne through open hole.

—IL linebacker Dana Howard (one tackle away from setting the all-time Big Ten record of 573) rushes up to tackle Milne at the goal line, and Milne blasts through as both players land in the end zone with 0:57 on the clock.

—Touchdown! 14 plays. 96 yards. Time consumed: 5:10.

to set its defense. Up in the TV booth, Brent Musburger told his audience, "Should Penn State pull this out, they've got to consider moving them back to No. 1."

In went a second tight end and fullback. Milne took the handoff and followed his blockers over the goal line through right tackle. The Lions bench exploded, but 57 seconds remained. Illinois hurried downfield on a flurry of passes against the prevent defense and reached the State 31 before Kim Herring intercepted a Hail Mary shot into the end zone with two seconds left.

Of course, the Lions went on to beat Oregon in the Rose Bowl, but they couldn't beat the pollsters and finished No. 2 behind Nebraska. Without "the Drive" they wouldn't even have done that.

January 1, 1969

The 12ᵗʰ Man

Lions Win Orange Bowl on Chuck Burkhart's Ad-Lib Touchdown and Kansas Penalty

Penn State's incredible come-from-behind 15–14 victory over Kansas in the final two minutes of the 1969 Orange Bowl is immortalized as "the 12ᵗʰ Man" game because of the Kansas penalty on a failed pass attempt for two points that gave the Nittany Lions a second chance to win the game. That penalty with seconds left and the subsequent successful run by tailback Bobby Campbell for the two winning points were the biggest plays of the game, but there was actually a sequence of momentous plays in the last 1:14 that was equally crucial to the final outcome.

The coaches as well as the media predicted a high-scoring game despite the strength of the teams' defensive units. But outsiders figured the Lions' outstanding defense, which gave up just 10.6 points per game compared to the Jayhawks 17.5, might be the difference, and Penn State was a slight favorite.

The game was a defensive battle from the start, with Kansas taking a 7–0 first-quarter lead. Penn State tied it up in the second quarter on six running plays from its own 47-yard line with junior tailback Charlie Pittman going up the middle 13 yards for the touchdown.

State came close again early in the third quarter with a time-consuming 66-yard drive to the half-inch line, but Kansas held on fourth down. The goal-line stand changed the momentum of the game, and in the opening series of the fourth quarter, Kansas forced the Lions to punt from their own 13. Jayhawks speedster Donnie Shanklin took the punt at the Kansas 47 and raced to the State 7 before Pittman dragged him down. Sophomore John Riggins went the rest of the way on two carries, and Kansas led 14–7.

Minutes later they were pounding at the goal again after a drive from their own 28-yard line. With a fourth-and-goal at the 1-yard line and 10 minutes still left in the game, Kansas coach Pepper Rodgers passed up a sure field goal and sent Riggins into the line, but he was brought down for no gain. For the next eight minutes the teams battled in Penn State territory until a punt gave the Jayhawks the ball

The infamous "12th Man" penalty against Kansas that gave Penn State a second chance to win the game with only seconds left. *Photo courtesy of the Penn State All-Sports Museum*

at their own 38 with two minutes remaining. Victory was within the Lions' reach with first down or maybe even a good deep punt.

Then came the greatest sequence of defensive and offensive plays in Penn State's football history. The Lions had all three timeouts left, and Paterno decided to use them to force a punt. On first down, end Lincoln Lippincott tackled quarterback Bobby Douglass for no gain. Then All-American tackle Mike Reid sacked Douglass twice for big losses, setting up a fourth-and-23 at the 25. Neal Smith crushed in to partially block the punt, and the ball went out at the 50 with 1:16 on the clock.

On the sideline, Paterno instructed junior quarterback Chuck Burkhart to avoid an interception but throw deep over Bobby Campbell's head so that they could fool Kansas and then come back on the next play over the middle to tight end Ted Kwalick. But returning to the huddle, Campbell, who was nursing an ankle injury, told Burkhart to "throw it to the left goal post, and I'll be there." Burkhart took the snap, and as he was about to be whacked by two Jayhawks, he heaved the ball. Campbell split between two defenders, snared the pass on the 20, and reached the 3-yard line before being tackled as the Penn State crowd came to life.

Penn State called its last timeout, and Paterno discussed a three-play series without a huddle, with the fullback Tom Cherry carrying twice and a third play Paterno would send in. Cherry was stopped twice for no gain, and Paterno called a scissors play right for Pittman with Campbell as a pass decoy on the left. At the line with 20 seconds remaining, Burkhart saw the defense edging toward the right and realized the play wouldn't work, but he had no time for an audible. So he faked to Pittman, kept the ball, and ran around the left end for the touchdown.

Paterno never liked ties, and he sent in a roll-out run-pass option with Kwalick at the goal and Campbell deep in the end zone as receivers. Two Kansas defenders knocked the ball away from Campbell, and the Kansas players and fans began to celebrate until the referee signaled a penalty for too many men on the field. Game films would later show that Kansas had 12 men on the field during the three previous plays too.

With a reprieve, Paterno sent in a play for a pitchout to Campbell going right, but when the referee held up the game because of the noise, Paterno switched to a Campbell sweep left. Campbell smashed between three Jayhawks and bulled across the goal line with eight seconds left on the clock.

As Paterno would often say in later years, "This Orange Bowl game put us on the map."

> **I** thought it up about the time I stepped back from center. It just came to me—I don't know why. I was supposed to hand the ball to Charlie Pittman...but I didn't; I just ran. I've never done anything like that before.
>
> —CHUCK BURKHART

Game Details

Penn State 15 • Kansas 14

Penn State	0	7	0	8	**15**
Kansas	7	0	0	7	**14**

Date: January 1, 1969

Team Records: Penn State 10–0, Kansas 9–1

Scoring Plays:

KAN—Reeves two-yard run (Bell PAT)
PSU—Pittman 13-yard run (Garthwaite PAT)
KAN—Riggins one-yard run (Bell PAT)
PSU—Burkhart three-yard run (Campbell run)

Chuck Burkhart

Sportswriters who covered the 1968 and 1969 Nittany Lions often criticized Chuck Burkhart, questioning his skills, consistently calling him erratic, and wondering why Paterno kept him in the lineup. It didn't help that he wore contact lenses while playing and wasn't especially fast on his feet or quick with his release on passing.

But as Coach Joe Paterno often pointed out, "all" Burkhart could do was win. Burkhart never lost one of the 42 games in which he started as quarterback from his high school days in suburban Pittsburgh through his final Penn State game in the 1970 Orange Bowl. "I stay with 'erratic' guys like that—consistently—because what they do consistently is lead teams to win football games," Paterno wrote in his 1989 book, *Paterno: By The Book*.

When Burkhart scored the last-second touchdown that enabled Penn State to beat Kansas, it was the first touchdown of his collegiate career. "I said I'd save my first touchdown for a time when it counted," he said after the game.

In 1969 Burkhart passed for two touchdowns and had 10 interceptions, but he did score two touchdowns, one of which helped beat Missouri, and his 11 completions in 26 attempts for 187 yards (and one interception) helped him win the Orange Bowl's Most Valuable Back Award.

Not bad for an "erratic" quarterback who could do nothing but win.

Chuck Burkhart's impromptu touchdown enables Penn State to come from behind and beat Kansas 15–14 in last minute of the 1969 Orange Bowl. *Photo courtesy of the Penn State All-Sports Museum*

Kirk "Stonehands" Bowman scores the first touchdown of his career in what many people call "the greatest game in Penn State history." *Photo courtesy of Penn State Athletic Communications*

September 25, 1982

McCloskey's Two-Step and Stonehands Bowman

Last-Minute Controversial Pass Receptions Help Upset Nebraska

Penn State's thrilling come-from-behind last-minute victory over Nebraska in the eerie but electrifying glow of unaccustomed to artificial lighting in Beaver Stadium in 1982 is regarded as the greatest game ever in the 50-year history of that facility.

A then-record crowd of 85,304 was there on a warm late afternoon, but nowadays thousands who watched the game on television or didn't even see it at all believe they were there. That's because the game has taken on a mystic quality, primarily because of the way it was won on a tense 10-play, 65-yard drive with 1:14 on the clock and the two controversial pass receptions in the last seconds that are still being talked about.

Few college stadiums had permanent lights as they do today, and when CBS-TV decided on a 3:45 PM kickoff—the latest start ever at Beaver Stadium—a bank of portable lights was set up over the press box.

The exhilarating pregame atmosphere was unlike anything ever seen before in Happy Valley, and the pumped-up partisan fans were on their feet cheering as the slightly underdog Lions jumped off to a surprising 14–0 lead six minutes into the second quarter on lengthy drives of 83 and 71 yards.

The Huskers didn't score until 38 seconds were left in the first half, when they went 80 yards on seven passes in about a minute. Nebraska missed a 35-yard field goal at the start of the third quarter, and as the portable lights suddenly went out, the Lions came back on another long, 83-yard drive to lead 21–7 with 5:18 gone in the second half.

Nebraska scored on a 15-play 80-yard drive with 3:28 remaining in the third quarter, and then two minutes into the final period they kicked a 37-yard field goal. But Blackledge soon had the Lions back in scoring territory until his pass into the end zone was intercepted just about the time the portable lights came back on.

There was 6:52 left on the clock, and Nebraska quarterback Tyler Gill used 5:34 of the time to take his team 80 yards on 13 plays and take the lead 24–21 as the dumbfounded Lions fans groaned.

Nebraska's kickoff went into the end zone, but a personal-foul penalty put the ball on the Lions' 35-yard line with 1:18 remaining and the Lions with no timeouts. "There was no panic," Blackledge said later. "Everybody was calm. We practice the two-minute drill every day."

In 26 seconds Blackledge threw two 16-yard passes to reach the Nebraska 33-yard line. A running play lost a yard, two pass attempts were incomplete, and with a fourth-and-11 and 32 seconds left, Paterno thought about a field goal to tie but wasn't confident in his freshman kicker. Blackledge scrambled to avoid a heavy rush and found Kenny Jackson on a curl pattern down the middle for 23 yards, and as soon as the clock restarted, Blackledge scrambled again and went out of bounds at the 17 with 13 seconds remaining.

The crowd was delirious as Blackledge took the snap and passed to starting tight end Mike McCloskey tiptoeing along the left sideline near the Nebraska bench. McCloskey grabbed the ball as he was going out of bounds at the 2. As the official signaled completion, the Huskers protested that McCloskey caught it out of bounds. Nine seconds remained.

State lined up in a full-house backfield with another pass play designed for McCloskey or the alternate receiver—second tight end Kirk Bowman, a converted lineman with the nickname "Stonehands," who had caught his first-ever pass in the first quarter for a touchdown. McCloskey was covered by two defenders, and Blackledge threw to Bowman near the back of the end zone. The ball was low, but Bowman dived, scooped the ball into his arms, and rolled on to the turf.

Penn State celebrates its thrilling, last-second, come-from-behind victory against Nebraska on September 25, 1982. *Photo courtesy of Penn State Athletic Communications*

The McCloskey Controversy

Mike McCloskey's sideline reception at Nebraska's 2-yard line with 13 seconds remaining has been frozen in controversy from the moment it happened.

The official did not hesitate in ruling a completed pass. At the time, videotape replays could not overturn an on-field decision, and it wasn't until the limited video angles were examined closely after the game that it appeared McCloskey was probably out of bounds.

More than 25 years later, McCloskey still isn't sure he was in bounds or out. "Quite honestly, it's hard for me to know," McCloskey said. "I was just catching the pass. It was pretty much bang-bang, and we had to hurry back to the huddle and get ready for the next play. At the time it didn't seem like much. It became bigger afterwards when people drew attention to the fact that it was a controversial call."

However, even if McCloskey had been ruled out of bounds, there was still time for Todd Blackledge to throw twice into the end zone from the 17-yard line. The real miracle was Kirk Bowman's shoestring catch for the winning touchdown. He was dropping so many passes in practice that his teammates nicknamed him "Stonehands." Bowman never had another catch that season and never scored another touchdown in his career.

As fans ran onto the field, the Huskers complained that the ball had touched the grass, and it took minutes before the Lions could try the extra point and tackle Mike Rozier on the kickoff to end the game. The fans stormed onto the field, tore down the goal posts, and milled around inside the stadium for a long time before celebrating into the night.

Video replays and game film would show that McCloskey was probably out of bounds on his reception, but Bowman's catch was good.

The Nittany Lions went on to win the national championship that year, but that wouldn't have happened without the receptions by McCloskey and Bowman. *Sports Illustrated* called the game, "The Miracle at Mount Nittany." And everyone in the world was there.

> **W**hen I let it go, I thought [Kirk] wouldn't be able to get it and was immediately thinking of what to call next.
>
> **—TODD BLACKLEDGE**

Game Details

Penn State 27 • Nebraska 24

Nebraska	0	7	7	10	**24**
Penn State	7	7	7	6	**27**

Date: September 25, 1982

Team Records: Penn State 3–0, Nebraska 2–0

Scoring Plays:

PSU—Bowman 14-yard pass from Blackledge (Manca PAT)

PSU—Warner two-yard run (Manca PAT)

NEB—Fryar 30-yard pass from Gill (Seibel PAT)

PSU—Jackson 18-yard pass from Blackledge (Manca PAT)

NEB—Rozier two-yard pass from Gill (Seibel PAT)

NEB—Seibel 37-yard FG

NEB—Gill one-yard run (Seibel PAT)

PSU—Bowman two-yard pass from Blackledge (kick failed)

October 15, 1994

Bringing the Big House Down

Late Fourth-Quarter Pass to Bobby Engram Beats Michigan and Vaults Lions to No. 1

In looking back at Penn State's memorable undefeated season of 1994, the thrilling 31–24 victory at Michigan on a glorious mid-October afternoon has somehow been overshadowed by other games later in the season. But if not for quarterback Kerry Collins' third-and-11, 16-yard touchdown pass to wideout Bobby Engram with 2:53 left in the game, nothing else would have mattered.

Just about everyone in the stadium known as "the Big House," including the Penn State and Michigan players, expected coach Joe Paterno to call for a field goal that would break the 24–24 tie and probably win the game. But Paterno, with a reputation for conservative play-calling and playing the percentages, ordered the surprising pass, and the Nittany Lions offense made it work.

That play—and Penn State's defensive clamp-down that followed to end any Michigan comeback—climaxed a game that lived up to expectations for the 106,832 who were part of what was then the third-largest crowd in college football history.

As the season progressed, the Lions had climbed from a preseason No. 9 to No. 3 behind a veteran offensive

team that overpowered five opponents by scoring no fewer than 38 points in a game. Michigan was still at its preseason rating of No. 5, despite losing a heartbreaking game to Colorado 27–26 on a 64-yard Hail Mary pass on the last play of the game just three weeks earlier in this same stadium. The Wolverines players swore they would not lose again in their Big House, and it was the home-stadium advantage that made Michigan a slight one-point favorite.

This was just the second season for Penn State in the Big Ten conference after 83 years of independence. The Lions were still upset at their frustrating 21–13 loss to Michigan at home the previous year and especially at the derogatory remarks by several Wolverines players about teaching some respect to the league's "11th" team. "You have to pay your dues," bragged star running back Tyrone Wheatley.

From the opening 3:30 PM kickoff, Penn State made Michigan pay for its insults, marching 73 yards on its first possession for a 24-yard field goal and building a 16–0 lead with less than six minutes left in the first half. But Michigan's defense and a crucial holding penalty that nullified a Ki-Jana Carter touchdown early in the second

Bobby Engram, seen here running on an end-around earlier in the 1994 Michigan game, scored the game-winning touchdown on a 16-yard pass reception late in the fourth quarter. *Photo courtesy of the Penn State Pattee-Paterno Library Sports Archives*

Kerry Collins' passing was instrumental in securing victory for Penn State over Michigan. *Photo courtesy of Penn State Athletic Communications*

quarter made the Lions settle for three field goals, and that came back to bite the Lions.

Throughout the first half, State's much-maligned defense had stymied Michigan. But with 10 seconds left in the half and the Wolverines bogged down at midfield, a third-down personal-foul penalty gave them new life, and their 33-yard field goal as time expired provided a spark for their second-half explosion.

Wheatley had been held to 11 yards on nine carries in the first half, but on the second play of the third quarter he bolted 67 yards for a touchdown. Minutes later, a shanked punt of just 16 yards gave Michigan the ball at its 49-yard line. Wheatley ran 21 yards for the touchdown, and suddenly the Wolverines led 17–16.

State immediately struck back with a 10-play 83-yard drive and two-point pass from Collins to Freddie Scott to regain the lead at 6:27 of the third quarter, but Michigan tied it up again about three minutes into the final period on a 59-yard drive. The game turned into a defensive battle as the teams exchanged punts until Penn State took the ball at its own 45 with 4:46 left in the game.

On first down, Engram barely got his left foot down as he went out of bounds at the right sideline on a leaping 14-yard catch, and then Carter blasted off tackle for 26 yards. Two plays lost one yard, and now everyone expected a short run toward the middle for a field-goal try. Instead, Engram found himself one-on-one with the cornerback on a

Joining the Big Ten

Although Penn State seemed like an outsider from the East when it began playing in the Big Ten conference in 1993, the Nittany Lions had ties to a couple of league teams that went back 70 years.

Despite what Penn State and Michigan may seem to have in common in sports and tradition, the teams had never met in football until their 1993 game at Beaver Stadium. But Michigan's biggest rival—Ohio State—first played Penn State in 1912, in Columbus, and the teams had played eight times—of which Penn State won six—before beginning formal Big Ten competition.

Penn State's second-longest Big Ten rival is Michigan State. They first met in 1914—a Friday the 13th, no less—in State College. They played nine more times between 1925 and 1966, and the Nittany Lions won only once (in 1925) and tied once.

When they first played Penn State, neither Ohio State nor Michigan State were formal members of the conference that would eventually become known as the Big Ten. The Lions' first game against an official league representative was in 1930 at Iowa. Penn State lost but won six of the next eight games with the Hawkeyes before 1993.

The Nittany Lions also had games in the 1950s, 1960s, and 1970s with Purdue, Wisconsin, and Illinois before joining the Big Ten.

post pattern, and he was wide open in the end zone when he caught Collins' pass.

But the game was far from over after Conway kicked the extra point. On the first play following the kickoff into the end zone, Wheatley went 30 yards to the 50. On third-and-1 at the State 41, linebacker Willie Smith stopped Tim Biakabutuka for no gain, and on fourth down cornerback Brian Miller intercepted a pass at the 28 with 1:28 remaining, and the Lions ran out the clock.

"The New Big Boys of the Big Ten," blared the headline in the *Chicago Sun-Times*, and two days later Penn State jumped to No. 1 in both major polls. Engram's touchdown helped do it, and it's too bad far too many Penn State fans have forgotten about it.

> **I**t's just unbelievable. I saw the ball in the air, and I knew that I had to make the big catch.... On that last drive, we were moving the ball well, and that's what they had to do. It was a great call.
>
> —BOBBY ENGRAM

Game Details

Penn State 31 • Michigan 24

Penn State	10	6	8	7	**31**
Michigan	0	3	14	7	**24**

Date: October 15, 1994

Team Records: Penn State 5–0, Michigan 4–1

Scoring Plays:

PSU—Conway 24-yard FG

PSU—Olsommer three-yard pass from Collins (Conway PAT)

PSU—Conway 28-yard FG

PSU—Conway 29-yard FG

UM—Hamilton 33-yard FG

UM—Wheatley 67-yard run (Hamilton PAT)

UM—Wheatley 21-yard run (Hamilton PAT)

PSU—Witman nine-yard pass from Collins (Collins pass to Scott)

UM—Biakabutuka one-yard run (Hamilton PAT)

PSU—Engram 16-yard pass from Collins (Conway PAT)

September 29, 1967

Paterno's Turning Point in Miami

Bobby Campbell's 35-Yard Run Helps Save Struggling Coaching Career

Joe Paterno has often said the 17–8 upset at Miami in the second game of his second year as Penn State's head coach saved his now-revered career. And the unbelievable 35-yard run by Bobby Campbell in the muggy Friday-night heat and rain of Orange Bowl Stadium is the play that did it.

It has been ingrained in the Paterno legend that the pivotal victory over Miami was accomplished by Paterno's gut decision earlier that week to use the first minutes of the game to subtly replace some of his senior defensive starters with untested sophomores. The sophomores became the core of an extraordinary defense that would catapult the Nittany Lions into the elite of college football over the next three years and set the course of Penn State football for decades.

No doubt, the sophomore-laden defense dominated the Miami game and was the major factor behind the win. But Campbell's run late

in the second quarter that set up Penn State's first touchdown changed the atmosphere of the game, instilling a confident attitude in the young Nittany Lions. Both Paterno and Miami coach Charlie Tate called it the turning point.

Both teams had lost their opening game the previous Saturday. Penn State, coming off a 5–5 season in Paterno's first year, fell to Navy 23–22 at Annapolis when Paterno's wilting defense could not hold a five-point lead with 1:45 to go as Navy drove 78 yards for the winning touchdown. Miami, a top 10 preseason pick by the media, was upset at Northwestern 12–7 but was now an 11-point favorite over the Lions.

With his young team about to play its first game in the unaccustomed heat and humidity of Miami, Paterno used a little psychology for the trip south. Rather than fly down the day before, he brought the team to Miami the morning of the game. Then he made the players stay in their air-conditioned rooms at an airport hotel so that the first time they'd be fully

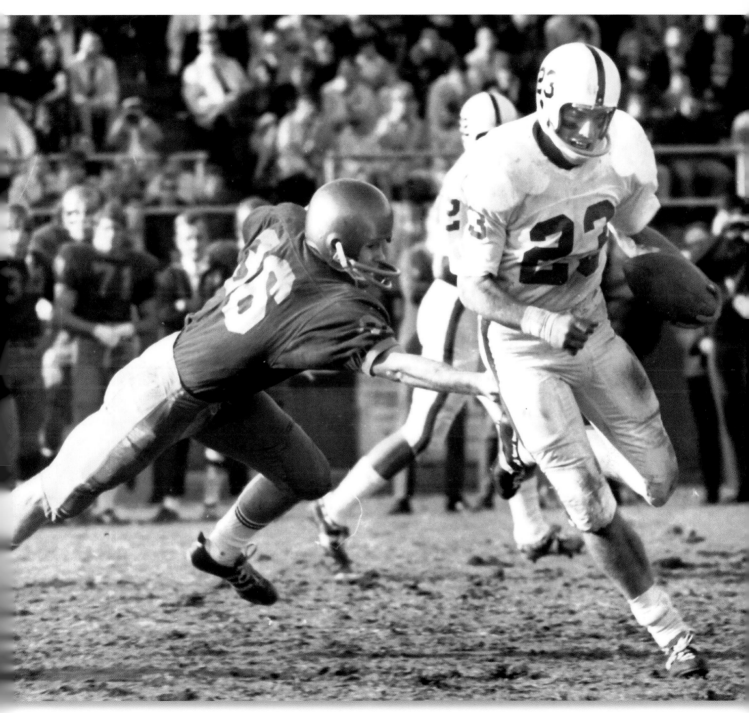

Bobby Campbell's spectacular running in 1967 helped turn around Joe Paterno's young coaching career.
Photo courtesy of the Penn State Pattee-Paterno Library Sports Archives

aware of the oppressive heat was when they stepped onto the field.

Paterno had another psychological ploy ready for the early moments of the game. Sophomore reserve tackle Steve Smear was already starting because of an injury during the Navy game. Paterno began subtly replacing some of his seniors one by one until several more sophomores who had not even practiced with the first team during the week were on the field. Linebacker Dennis Onkotz, who would eventually be a two-time All-American in 1968 and 1969, said later that he and the other sophomores were surprised to be playing that night.

With the sophomores still trying to adjust to the new 4-4-3 cover-2 mobile-zone defense Paterno had designed over the summer and was using for the first time in this game, the first half developed into a punting duel, with Campbell's high punts into Miami territory helping to

overcome the sputtering Lions offense. Then, with five minutes left in the second quarter and a steady drizzle continuing in the humid 78-degree temperature, the Lions took the ball at their own 27-yard line. With two quick passes they were at the 50.

On first down, quarterback Tom Sherman gave the ball to Campbell on a scissors play sweeping right. Miami's All-American end Ted Hendricks crashed in to make the tackle but was jostled by sophomore split end Paul Johnson, and Campbell cut left, evaded more tacklers at the line of scrimmage, and burst up the middle for about 10 yards. Then as he continued sidestepping, juking, and brushing away tacklers, he sped diagonally toward the left sideline until he was hauled out of bounds at the Miami 15.

On the next play, Sherman faked to both the halfback and fullback, took a step toward the line, then stopped and threw to tight end Ted Kwalick in the end zone. The

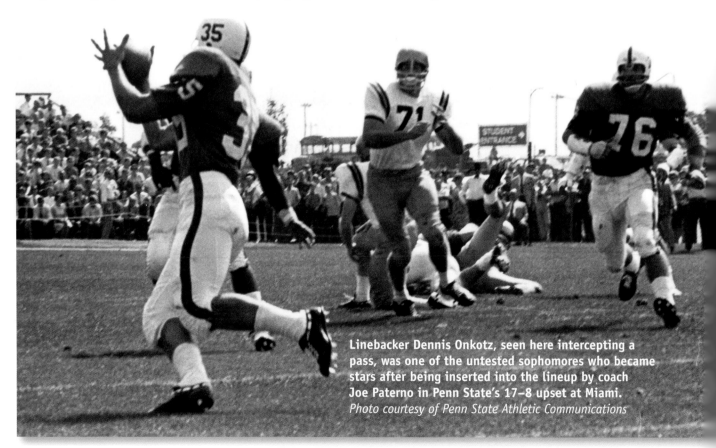

Linebacker Dennis Onkotz, seen here intercepting a pass, was one of the untested sophomores who became stars after being inserted into the lineup by coach Joe Paterno in Penn State's 17–8 upset at Miami.
Photo courtesy of Penn State Athletic Communications

Bobby Campbell: The Forgotten Running Back

Bobby Campbell was the first of coach Joe Paterno's great running backs, but his name is rarely mentioned nowadays by the current generation of Penn State football fans.

When Campbell helped turn around Paterno's career at Miami, Paterno told sportswriters after the game that Campbell was "one of the finest players I've ever coached. He is a great all-around back, and he can do almost anything."

The previous season, Campbell had become the first sophomore since Lenny Moore in 1953 to lead Penn State in rushing with 482 yards and five touchdowns on 79 carries for a 6.1-yards-per-carry average.

Campbell is still ranked 24th in the Lions' career rushing category—with 1,480 yards on 242 attempts and 14 touchdowns—and 15th in 100-yard rushing games with six.

Campbell's best game ever was his last in the regular season of 1968 when he ran for 239 yards and two touchdowns on 24 attempts and caught three passes for another 20 yards in a 30–12 victory over Syracuse. Less than a month later Campbell helped bring Penn State from behind in the last minute of the 1969 Orange Bowl to beat Kansas.

Campbell may not be remembered among Penn State's greatest running backs, but he should be. There was no one better when everything was on the line.

As Joe Paterno once said, "Bobby Campbell made us a winner."

---

extra-point kick was wide, but State had the lead and the momentum.

The Lions controlled the rest of the game on offense and defense, building up a 17–0 lead and stopping Miami's only serious threat on four downs at the PSU 8-yard line with five minutes left in the game. The Hurricanes finally scored with 47 seconds remaining when Campbell went back to punt on a fourth-and-3 at the Lions' 24 and thought he saw an opening to run instead of punt. But he changed his mind near the line of scrimmage, and the ball went off the end of his foot. Miami recovered and passed for a touchdown, but the game was over. Joe Paterno's coaching career was saved, and then some.

> The run by Campbell really picked us up. We had trouble moving the ball until then, but after that the boys knew we could go all the way on one play.
>
> —JOE PATERNO

Game Details

Penn State 17 • Miami 8

Penn State	0	6	8	3	**17**
Miami	0	0	0	8	**8**

Date: September 29, 1967

Team Records: Penn State 0–1, Miami 0–1

Scoring Plays:

PSU—Kwalick 15-yard pass from Sherman (kick failed)

PSU—Abbey seven-yard pass from Sherman (Curry pass from Sherman)

PSU—Abbey 24-yard FG

MIA—Cox 24-yard pass from Miller (DeRoss pass from Miller)

September 24, 2005

Mike-Rob Saves the Season and Football Program

Michael Robinson's Late Fourth-Quarter Comeback at Northwestern

Derrick Williams scores the first touchdown of his career after making a dramatic fourth-quarter catch to beat Northwestern 34–29. *Photo courtesy of* Blue White Illustrated *and Harvey Levine*

No one believed Coach Joe Paterno or his players in the summer of 2005 when they said they had a team that could win the Big Ten title and make a run at the national championship. With just one winning season since 1999, the Nittany Lions had plummeted sharply into their worst stretch of mediocrity since the non-scholarship de-emphasis period of the 1930s.

But in a desperate, tension-filled span of about 100 seconds on an overcast late-September day at Northwestern's Ryan Field, the underrated 2005 team reversed the course of Penn State's entire football program behind the imperfect throwing arm of gutsy senior quarterback Michael Robinson. No one could have predicted what he did with 1:39 left in the game on that early afternoon in Evanston.

Neither team was ranked among the top 25 in the preseason polls. Both were picked to finish in the lower half of the Big Ten, and this was their first conference game. Although the undefeated

Nittany Lions were favored by a touchdown, they had won only one of eight conference road games in the last two years and were 6–20 away from Beaver Stadium since 2000.

Penn State was listless and sloppy throughout the first half, with even Northwestern's special teams pulling off a successful onside kick and fake punt to embarrass the visitors. Robinson, in particular, was horrible. He threw three interceptions—two of them bouncing off receivers—and fumbled three times, losing one inside the Northwestern 5-yard line, as the Wildcats took a shocking 23–7 lead in the second quarter before a Robinson touchdown pass to freshman Deon Butler made it 23–14 only 35 seconds before halftime.

"You turn the ball over that many times on the road, and you're usually going to get your ears pinned," Paterno said later.

Although the defense also staggered through an erratic first half, giving up 276 yards to the aggressive Wildcats, it forced the home team to kick three field goals instead of scoring touchdowns. That would be crucial for what happened in the last two minutes of the fourth quarter.

The Lions looked liked a different team in the second half, and with less than nine minutes left in the game, they stormed back on a 77-yard drive to go ahead 27–26. But Northwestern countered with its own 86-yard drive—aided by a questionable 15-yard penalty on an out-of-bounds tackle at the Wildcats' 10-yard line on a third-and-13 that kept the drive alive—and grabbed the lead again, 29–27, on a 25-yard field goal.

Northwestern kicked off into the end zone, and there was 2:10 remaining when Penn State gained possession at its own 20-yard line. Robinson gathered the team on the sideline and said, "This is what we wake up for, this is what we put all our time in for, games like this."

Michael Robinson

Michael Robinson was recruited out of Richmond, Virginia, primarily as a running and passing quarterback, but he was such a gifted natural athlete that Paterno wanted him on the field as a redshirt freshman. He not only played quarterback but also running back, receiver, and kick-returner, and that trend continued for the next two years.

Yet despite his proven versatility, there were some in the media who felt Robinson's quarterback skills were inadequate over the course of a season. In the preseason Big Ten hype of 2005, Robinson was virtually ignored.

After leading the Lions to the Big Ten Championship and the Orange Bowl, Robinson won the prestigious Chicago Tribune Silver Football as the Big Ten's Most Valuable Player, was deemed the Big Ten Offensive Player of the Year by the league coaches, and finished eighth in the Heisman Trophy voting. Robinson had also fared well in the classroom, earning his second undergraduate degree in December and becoming a four-time Big Ten Academic All-American.

Leave it up to Paterno to have the final words once again. As he told the media a few hours after the Orange Bowl victory that gave Penn State an 11–1 record and No. 3 final ranking in the polls, "Michael Robinson is one of the strongest leaders I have ever had."

Joe Paterno called Michael Robinson one of the most versatile athletes in the country from 2003 to 2005 and one of the best leaders in Penn State history.
Photo courtesy of Steve Manuel

But three plays later, including another fumble by Robinson, the Lions were backed up to their own 15-yard line and facing a seemingly last-gasp fourth-and-15 with 1:39 left on the clock. After a timeout, the coaches in the press box sent in the play: "Four Vertical."

Robinson took the snap, and just as it looked like he would be tackled, he threw the ball to tight end Isaac Smolko, who was wide open over the middle for a 20-yard gain. "In practice, we hit it every single time," Robinson after the game. "Smolko gets it every single time."

With no timeouts left, Robinson threw for two first downs, reaching the Northwestern 40, and then was nearly sacked but squirmed away for a four-yard gain to the Wildcats' 36. Now it was third-and-6 with 51 seconds remaining, and the Northwestern defense poised for an all-out, nine-man rush. Penn State's talented freshman receiver, Derrick Williams, the No. 1 high school recruit in the country just months before, flanked left, covered alone by the safety.

Robinson took the snap, and just a split second before he was buried by two linebackers, he threw toward Williams speeding down the left sideline. "I saw Mike start to run, and I'm yelling, 'Throw it! Get rid of it!'" said Paterno afterward.

The blitz caused Robinson to hurry the pass, and it was slightly underthrown. But Williams caught the ball as he crossed the 10-yard line, ducked under the safety trying to tackle him, and went into the end zone for the first touchdown of his career.

Northwestern had one more chance after the Penn State kickoff, but cornerback Anwar Phillips' interception at the Penn State 40 on the first play ended it all.

The dramatic fourth-quarter comeback spurred by Robinson's late-game heroics gave the Nittany Lions the momentum for one of the most gratifying years in school history and propelled Penn State back into the elite of college football.

> **I** was getting bracketed the whole game up to that point. But once I saw that one-on-one, I said, "It might be my turn, this play right here." And that's what I did. There really wasn't an adjustment. I just saw the ball in the air, and I just tried to go get it.
>
> —DERRICK WILLIAMS

Game Details

Penn State 34 • Northwestern 29

Penn State	0	14	3	17	**34**
Northwestern	10	13	0	6	**29**

Date: September 24, 2005

Team Records: Penn State 3–0, Northwestern 2–1

Scoring Plays:

NW—Sutton one-yard run (Howells PAT)

NW—Howells 20-yard FG

NW—Howells 25-yard FG

PSU—King 37-yard pass from Robinson (Kelly PAT)

NW—Sutton one-yard run (Howells PAT)

NW—Howells 42-yard FG

PSU—Butler 26-yard pass from Robinson (Kelly PAT)

PSU—Kelly 25-yard FG

PSU—Kelly 28-yard FG

NW—Howells 46-yard FG

PSU—Robinson eight-yard run (Kelly PAT)

NW—Howells 25-yard FG

PSU—Williams 36-yard pass from Robinson (Kelly PAT)

November 24, 1978

A Little White Lie for a Chance at the National Championship

Lions Pass Up Field Goal and Score Touchdown to Remain No. 1

For the first time in 91 years of playing college football, Penn State was on the field as the nation's No. 1 team. If State could defeat Pitt at Beaver Stadium on this chilly and windy Friday after Thanksgiving, it would become Joe Paterno's fourth undefeated and untied team in his 13 years as Penn State's head coach. But this would be the first with the opportunity to earn the national title on the field after his other teams in 1968, 1969, and 1973 had been snubbed in the final polls.

Ten days earlier, after defeating heavy underdog North Carolina State in a close game on this same field, the Lions had been voted No. 1 for the first time. Then six days prior, they accepted an invitation to the Sugar Bowl to play the Southeast Conference champion. All No. 2 Alabama had to do to be there was beat a weak Auburn team on December 2. Even if Alabama lost, and then No. 13 Georgia became the opponent, a Lions victory in the Sugar Bowl would almost guarantee the championship because Penn State would be the only undefeated team in the country.

The oddsmakers made Penn State a 17-point favorite. But the 77,465 hearty, bundled-up fans that filed into Beaver Stadium—with temperatures in the low 20s and winds gusting from 15 to 25 miles an hour—knew Pitt would not go quietly. The combativeness started 90 minutes before the kickoff when Paterno complained about the length of the cleats on the shoes the Panthers would be wearing and the game officials went into the locker room for inspection. They found nothing wrong. But after the game, Pitt's second-year coach Jackie Sherrill angrily accused Paterno of "unethical" conduct.

It was a defensive battle all the way, but right from the start the high-powered Lions offense was on the attack, fumbling away two scoring chances inside the Pitt 20 before Mike Guman bolted over the left tackle from the 3-yard line and Matt Bahr's extra point made it 7–0. The Panthers took advantage of a short State punt into the wind to tie the game in the second quarter and used the wind and an interception in the third period to go ahead 10–7 on a 27-yard field goal with 6:32 left.

Mike Guman was the workhorse runner in this 1978 Pitt game, carrying the ball 15 times for 43 yards and scoring both touchdowns in the come-from-behind 17–10 victory. *Photo courtesy of Penn State Athletic Communications*

After appearing on the *Bob Hope Show* featuring the AP All-American team, quarterback Chuck Fusina and his wife were invited to a private dinner at the Hope mansion. *Photo courtesy of Penn State Athletic Communications*

From that point on it was a fight for field position, and Penn State used a methodical grind-it-out offense to control the tempo of the game. State attempted a field goal from the Pitt 41 but lost the ball on a bad snap. Moments later, the wind held up a Pitt punt, and the Lions took possession at the Panther 42-yard line. Six plays later, the Lions were inside the 4 with a fourth-down-and-short and 5:02 left in the game.

The field-goal unit started onto the field but was called back when Paterno asked for a timeout because he couldn't see the ball from the sideline. He said he wanted to go for a first down, but one assistant had told him it was four yards away, another said two yards, and a third said one. So, as Paterno huddled with his offense, he sent the one man he could trust to tell him the truth: quarterback Chuck Fusina. Fusina returned holding his hands about a foot or so apart.

"I lied a little," Fusina said after the game. It was actually two yards. "I expected to do a fake roll where I fake to a back up the middle and roll out." But Paterno called "40 Pitch." Pitt figured it would be a typical Penn State goal-line run up the middle.

Fusina took the snap and pitched to Guman going left. The Pitt end went outside, and Guman cut inside

"Nobody Remembers Who Finishes Second"

Chuck Fusina had the misfortune of being the quarterback on the Penn State team that lost the national championship in a heartbreaking loss to Alabama in the 1979 Sugar Bowl. If not for that, maybe it would be Fusina's photo on the cover of *Sports Illustrated* that everyone would remember, not just Gregg Garrity's from the 1983 Sugar Bowl or Todd Blackledge's from the 1982 Nebraska game.

Neither Garrity nor Blackledge came as close to winning the Heisman Trophy as Fusina did. Garrity didn't receive a vote in 1982 when Blackledge finished sixth with 108 votes, 1,818 behind Georgia's Herschel Walker. Curt Warner also had 40 votes that year.

Fusina, who was the *Sports Illustrated* cover boy at midseason when Penn State was closing in to being No. 1 for the first time in history, missed the Heisman

> **A**ll I was concerned with was getting the ball out to him because when it's windy the ball really flies. As soon as I pitched it I saw their end coming out, and it was clear. I think I knew it would go in.
>
> —CHUCK FUSINA

Trophy by just 77 votes. He was the runner-up to Oklahoma's Billy Sims in what was then the closest voting in 14 years. Fusina did win the Maxwell Club Award in 1978 as the "outstanding player in collegiate football" and was the consensus All-American quarterback.

"Nobody remembers who finishes second," Fusina once said, "whether it's the Heisman Trophy, the national championship game, or the Super Bowl, but that's just how it is."

as guard Eric Cunningham wiped out the halfback and Matt Suhey knocked down the linebacker. Tackle Keith Dorney and tight end Irv Pankey sealed off the inside and helped make a hole so wide Guman went into the end zone untouched. Bahr's extra point made it 14–10. "We used that play a lot. It was up to Mike to cut where he sees the crack, and the crack opened inside," Paterno said later.

As darkness started to envelop Beaver Stadium, linebacker Rich Milot intercepted a Pitt pass that set up a 38-yard field goal, and moments later linebacker Lance Mehl's interception at the Panthers' 40 ended the game.

On December 2, Alabama beat Auburn, and Penn State had its winner-take-all game at the Sugar Bowl on January 1, 1979. Unfortunately, that turned into one of the most crushing and disheartening losses in Penn State's football history, and because of how it ended, Guman's crucial run against State's biggest rival and Fusina's little white lie have been virtually forgotten.

Game Details

Penn State 17 • Pitt 10

Pittsburgh	0	7	3	0	**10**
Penn State	7	0	0	10	**17**

Date: November 24, 1978

Team Records: Penn State 10–0, Pitt 8–2

Scoring Plays:

PSU—Guman three-yard run (Bahr PAT)

PITT—Gaustad 16-yard pass from Trocano (Schubert PAT)

PITT—Schubert 27-yard FG

PSU—Guman four-yard run (Bahr PAT)

PSU—Bahr 38-yard FG

Ki-Jana Carter's 83-yard touchdown run on Penn State's first offensive play in the 1995 Rose Bowl is one of the most dramatic plays in the history of Penn State football. *Photo courtesy of Penn State Athletic Communications*

January 2, 1995

Ki-Jana's Run for the Roses

Carter's 83-Yard Touchdown Ignites Rose Bowl Win, but Two Little-Known Reserves Save Game

The most memorable moment in Penn State's 1995 Rose Bowl victory over Oregon is Ki-Jana Carter's startling 83-yard touchdown run on the Lions' first offensive play of the game. Yet, that was not the most consequential play in the 38–20 victory.

Actually, there were two plays late in the third quarter by two little-known reserves that were the catalyst for the win—a kickoff return and an interception. The plays woke up a listless, disappointed team that was not playing well and saved what would have been an embarrassing and disastrous end to one of the greatest seasons in Penn State history.

The tale of the 1994 team's exceptional undefeated season and its controversial rejection by the pollsters for the national championship is a familiar one to Nittany Lions fans. En route to their first Big Ten championship and Rose Bowl victory, the Lions had overwhelmed all of their foes and set NCAA records for total offense (520.2 yards per game) and scoring (47.8 points a game). But from about midseason, the voters favored Nebraska, and when the Huskers beat Miami in the Orange Bowl on New Year's night, the Lions realized they had no chance to become No. 1 even if they clobbered Oregon the next afternoon in Pasadena.

Penn State's defense seemed jittery at the start when Oregon took the opening kickoff and used up six minutes of the clock. But the defense forced a punt at the State 48-yard line, and the Lions' potent offense took over at the 17-yard line. In 10 explosive seconds, Penn State had the lead as Carter bolted off the edge of the Lions' right end on their first play, broke two tackles near the line of scrimmage, and was in the clear at the 28-yard line before the Ducks

Sophomore Joe Jurevicius catches one of his two crucial passes in Penn State's 38–20 victory over Oregon in the 1995 Rose Bowl. *Photo courtesy of Getty Images*

Game Details

Penn State 38 • Oregon 20

Penn State	7	7	14	10	**38**
Oregon	7	0	7	6	**20**

Date: January 2, 1995

Team Records: Penn State 11–0, Oregon 9–3

Scoring Plays:

PSU—Carter 83-yard run (Conway PAT)

ORE—Wilcox one-yard pass from O'Neil (Belden PAT)

PSU—Milne one-yard run (Conway PAT)

ORE—McLemore 17-yard pass from O'Neil (Belden PAT)

PSU—Carter 17-yard run (Conway PAT)

PSU—Carter three-yard run (Conway PAT)

PSU—Conway 43-yard FG

PSU—Witman nine-yard run (Barninger PAT)

ORE—Whittle three-yard run (pass failed)

knew what hit them. To Penn State fans who had witnessed similar dramatic touchdowns earlier in the season, it looked as if the Lions were going to take all of their frustration out on the 17-point-underdog Ducks. But in less than a minute, Oregon went 80 yards in four plays to tie it, and Oregon became the aggressor into the third quarter.

Three times in the first half Oregon drove deep into State territory but missed two field goals and also lost the ball at the State 9 on an interception by redshirt sophomore Chuck Penzenik. Penzenik, a heretofore fourth-string cornerback who had been switched to starting free safety because of injuries when the team arrived in California, would make the biggest play of the game in the second half.

With 3:48 left in the second quarter, State's offense perked up and drove 73 yards on seven plays, including a crucial 44-yard pass to sophomore Joe Jurevicius, to regain the lead 14–7 with 1:26 remaining. However, Oregon responded with its own hurry-up 73-yard march to the State 9-yard line with 11 seconds left, but time ran out when quarterback Danny O'Neil completed a four-yard pass over the middle instead of throwing the ball out of bounds. "That was a killer," Oregon coach Rich Brooks said later.

Ki-Jana Carter

Ki-Jana Carter is one of Penn State's greatest running backs. If not for what happened beyond his control, Carter might be ranked among the all-time best in football, right up there with such Heisman Trophy winners and All-Pros as Barry Sanders, O.J. Simpson, and Tony Dorsett.

Unfortunately, he finished second to Colorado's Rashaan Salaam in the 1994 Heisman voting, and many Nittany Lions fans still believe Carter lost because of the same media bias against Penn State that denied the team at least a share of the national championship that year. There also was the fact that he was competing against his talented teammate, quarterback Kerry Collins, who finished fourth.

But what really tarnished Carter's national legacy was his ill-fated professional career. Leaving Penn State after his redshirt junior season, he was the first player selected in the 1995 NFL draft, when picked No. 1 by the Cincinnati Bengals. The Pro Football Hall of Fame seemed to be his destiny.

Carter's path to Canton virtually ended the third time he carried the ball, in a preseason game at Detroit. He tore an ACL in his left knee; missed the entire season; and was never the same explosive, shifty, and speedy runner he had been in college. Carter bounced around the league for nearly 10 years, struggling with a couple more injuries, and finished his NFL career with just 1,127 yards and 20 touchdowns.

State was in trouble again after the second-half kickoff when quarterback Kerry Collins threw his only interception of the day and Oregon ran it back 38 yards to the State 17. Two plays later the Ducks tied it again, and with just 4:54 gone in the quarter, Oregon seemed to have the momentum back.

But moments later, redshirt freshman Ambrose Fletcher, the backup tailback to Carter and Mike Archie, took the kickoff at the 7-yard line, found a seam, and raced into the clear down the right sideline until tackled from behind at the Oregon 21. Carter did the rest in two plays,

scoring on a 17-yard touchdown run around his left end. "That was the spark. That was a wake-up call," said Lions receiver Bobby Engram, who had won the first Biletnikoff Award as the nation's outstanding receiver a few days earlier.

On Oregon's next series, Penzenik picked off an O'Neil pass at the State 43 and didn't stop running until grabbed from behind at the Oregon 13. Three plays later Carter ran in from the 3 for a 28–14 lead, and the demoralized Ducks were never in the game again. "Unlikely Safety Saves Day," read the headline in the *Los Angeles Times* the next day.

Five of those 1994 talented Nittany Lions were first-round NFL draft choices, and more than a half-dozen others played several years in the NFL, including Collins, Engram, and Jurevicius, who were still going strong in 2008. That offense was one of college football's all-time best. Yet if not for two clutch plays by a couple of obscure reserves it all might have ended with a thud. Sometimes great plays are made by ordinary players when least expected.

> **I** read the quarterback all the way. I saw it coming and I thought I was going all the way, but one of their guys ran me down. It was the first time I'd run that far since I was an all-state running back in high school."
>
> **—CHUCK PENZENIK**

November 2, 1968

Kwalick's Onside Kickoff Return

Ted Kwalick's Bizarre Fourth-Quarter Touchdown Keeps Nittany Lions Undefeated

Like many special-teams plays in the history of college football, Ted Kwalick's return of an onside kick for a touchdown late in the fourth quarter to beat Army in 1968 had repercussions for decades. If Penn State had not defeated Army that day in Beaver Stadium, the Nittany Lions would not have gone unbeaten in the regular season and probably would not have played in the Orange Bowl on New Year's night.

One can not say for certain that the success that came after Penn State's thrilling come-from-behind win over Kansas in the Orange Bowl would not have occurred in the subsequent years. But no doubt the Nittany Lions' course to the top of the college football world would have been altered, and the enduring legacy of the 1968 team as one of Penn State's greatest would not exist.

This was game six of 1968, and the Lions were hot, moving from a No. 10 preseason ranking to No. 4 with overwhelming victories. They were averaging 27 points a game, and only one opponent had scored more than nine

points. Despite a respectable 4–2 record, Army was a two-touchdown underdog, but Penn State had never beaten the Cadets at Beaver Field in three games dating to 1957, and Army led in the overall rivalry series at 10–4–2.

The year 1968 saw an abundance of protests over the Vietnam War, and dozens of Penn State students demonstrated that weekend against the appearance of army chief of staff General William Westmoreland. But there were no major incidents around the stadium, even with the appearance of 1,200 West Point cadets and their irritating, shrieking air horns.

It was Homecoming Day, and the sellout crowd of 49,653 expected a relatively relaxing afternoon despite the wind and chill. In the first quarter, Penn State took the opening kickoff and went downfield into the wind, primarily on the running of Bobby Campbell and Charlie Pittman. Campbell, the team's leading runner, had missed the last three games because of injuries, but he was back in form and scored the touchdown from nine yards out on a double reverse.

This touchdown reception by Ted Kwalick in the 1967 milestone win over North Carolina State (see page 72) helped set Penn State's career touchdown record of 10 for tight ends that has stood for 40 years. *Photo courtesy of Penn State Athletic Communications*

After the ensuing kickoff, the Lions forced a punt from the Army 29, and the snap sailed over punter Charlie Jarvis' head. Jarvis retrieved the ball in the end zone and knelt down for a safety, giving State a 9–0 lead. But Army regrouped, going 87 yards for its own touchdown early in the second quarter and stopping the Lions four times within the Cadets' 20-yard line during the half.

The Lions widened their lead on their first possession of the second half, driving from midfield for a touchdown, but a Cadets field goal four minutes into the fourth quarter made the score 16–10. Then came the second-biggest play of the game. After a Penn State drive stalled at the Army 21, the Lions tried a field goal into the wind, but the ball was short. However, the Army safety inadvertently kicked the ball, and Lions tackle John Kulka fell on it at the 2. Three plays later, Campbell scored the touchdown, but a two-point pass for the extra points failed.

With about four minutes left in the game, the partisan crowd relaxed. But on the second play after the kickoff, Army's veteran quarterback Steve Lindell and receiver Gary Steele hooked up on a 58-yard bomb to State's 5-yard line, and four plays later the score was 22–17 with 2:29 remaining.

Onside kicks were an Army specialty, and during the week Penn State had practiced for this exact situation. Army's kick bounced toward the Lions' front line near the 50 along the Penn State sideline. Sophomore guard Charlie Zapiec tried to pick it up, but it rolled slowly toward tackle Dave Bradley, who appeared to have the ball in his grasp when several Army tacklers smashed into Zapiec and Bradley and they all went down in a heap. Suddenly, the ball squirted out.

"I was just standing there, and it popped into my hands, and I just took off and ran down the sidelines for a touchdown," Kwalick said later. He picked up the ball at Penn State's 47-yard line and was in the clear before anyone realized it. A pass for two failed again, but with 2:22 left, Army wasn't done. In seven quick plays, the Cadets scored a touchdown but kicked the extra point, rather than trying for two, and then lined up for another onside kick. This time Zapiec grabbed the ball tightly, and the Lions ran out the clock.

Penn State went on to four more decisive wins in the regular season and earned that invitation to its first New Year's Day game in 21 years at the Orange Bowl. But what if Army had recovered that onside kick instead of Kwalick?

> **I** saw Dave [Bradley] holding the ball between his legs. A Cadet punched it out of Dave's legs, and the ball popped out. I was just standing there and it popped into my hands, and I just took off and ran down the sidelines for a touchdown.
>
> —TED KWALICK

Game Details

Penn State 28 • Army 24

Army	0	7	0	17	**24**
Penn State	9	0	7	12	**28**

Date: November 2, 1968
Team Records: Penn State 5–0, Army 4–2

Scoring Plays:
PSU—Campbell nine-yard run (Garthwaite PAT)
PSU—Safety (Army recovers own fumble in end zone)
ARM—Moore 13-yard pass from Lindell (Jensen PAT)
PSU—Pittman one-yard run (Garthwaite PAT)
ARM—Jensen 30-yard FG
PSU—Campbell two-yard run (Pass failed)
ARM—Jarvis one-yard run (Jensen PAT)
PSU—Kwalick 53-yard return of onside kickoff (Pass failed)
ARM—Steele eight-yard pass from Lindell (Jensen PAT)

> **W**e worked on that play in practice. Bradley would kick it around, then kick it to Kwalick, who would run for the touchdown.
>
> —JOE PATERNO (PARTIALLY KIDDING)

Ted Kwalick

More than 40 years after he caught his last pass and made his last crucial block for Penn State in the 1969 Orange Bowl, Ted Kwalick is still considered the Nittany Lions' all-time-greatest tight end. Kwalick helped define the position during his three years as a starter on Joe Paterno's first teams from 1966 to 1968.

Paterno once said the 6'4", 230-pound Kwalick is "what God had in mind for a football player." Kwalick was the first Penn State junior selected as a first-team All-American, and he repeated in his senior season when he also finished fourth in the Heisman Trophy race. He also is one of just 18 Nittany Lions enshrined in the College Football Hall of Fame and the second player inducted (in 1989) from the Paterno era.

Kwalick still holds the Lions' career record for most receptions (86), yardage (1,343), and touchdowns (10) by a tight end. In his final Penn State game, at the 1969 Orange Bowl, he led all receivers with six catches for 74 yards, and on the last play of his career, his critical block helped Bobby Campbell score a two-point conversion that beat Kansas 15–14.

Two-time first-team All-American Ted Kwalick is considered the greatest tight end in Penn State football history and was enshrined in the College Football Hall of fame in 1989. *Photo courtesy of AP Images*

January 1, 1974

Cappelletti and the One-Handed Pass Reception

Pass Reception and Punt Return Beats LSU in Orange Bowl

Joe Paterno's underrated and under-appreciated 1973 team was his third in six years that won all its games but was ranked below No. 1 at the end of the season.

This was also John Cappelletti's team, and he won the Heisman Trophy as college football's outstanding player, becoming the first and still only Penn State player to receive the prestigious award.

Yet the play of the year did not involve Cappelletti but was the handiwork of a dexterous wide receiver named Chuck Herd, who was overshadowed by one of his more productive pass-catching teammates, Gary Hayman. It happened New Year's night in the Orange Bowl.

Despite accolades for Cappelletti, the media demeaned the 1973 team throughout the season, constantly criticizing the schedule even as the Lions overwhelmed their opponents. With No. 1 Alabama virtually picking its opponent, No. 3 Notre Dame, for the national championship game in the Sugar Bowl

on New Year's Eve, No. 6 Penn State was matched in late November with No. 13 and twice-beaten LSU in the Orange Bowl.

Even before kickoff, Penn State knew its chances for moving much further up in the polls were practically nil. But these Nittany Lions weren't about to give their critics any satisfaction, even though they got off to a sluggish start.

Just as a heavy rain shower was ending, LSU ran back the opening kickoff to midfield and scored a touchdown nine plays and three minutes later. That quick strike seemed to wake up the Lions. LSU had just four more serious scoring opportunities the rest of the evening, including one early in the third quarter when it picked up its final two points on a safety after the Lions muffed a punt attempt near the end zone.

In fact, if not for a blown call by the officials in the first half, Penn State's margin of victory might have been higher. Toward the end of the first quarter, Chris Bahr kicked what was then an Orange Bowl–record

Heisman Trophy winner John Cappelletti scores Penn State's game-clinching touchdown to defeat LSU 16–9 in the 1974 Orange Bowl and finish the season undefeated. *Photo courtesy of Penn State Athletic Communications*

44-yard field goal. LSU responded by quickly moving into range for a long field goal at the State 44-yard line. The Lions blocked the kick, and on the first play from the LSU 35, Tom Shuman found Herd deep in the end zone. The officials ruled Herd was out of bounds, although TV replays showed he had one foot inside.

LSU forced a punt but then had to punt the ball back. Hayman was the nation's leading punt-return man, and he caught the ball near the Lions' 23-yard line, slipped almost to his knees on the wet Poly-turf, caught his balance, and was in the clear at the LSU 25. But he was halted by an official who claimed his knee had touched the ground.

Again TV replays showed otherwise, but it didn't matter two plays later.

On second down from the State 28-yard line, Shuman heaved a long, high pass to Herd streaking down the right sideline. As Herd was passing the LSU defender at the Tigers' 35-yard line at full speed, he reached up high and caught the ball on the fingertips of his left hand, somehow pulled it into the crook of his arm, clutched it with his right arm, and ran for a touchdown.

"I kind of cradled it in my left hand, grabbed it with my right, and tried to get into the end zone," he said in the locker room. "Frankly, I thought it was out of reach."

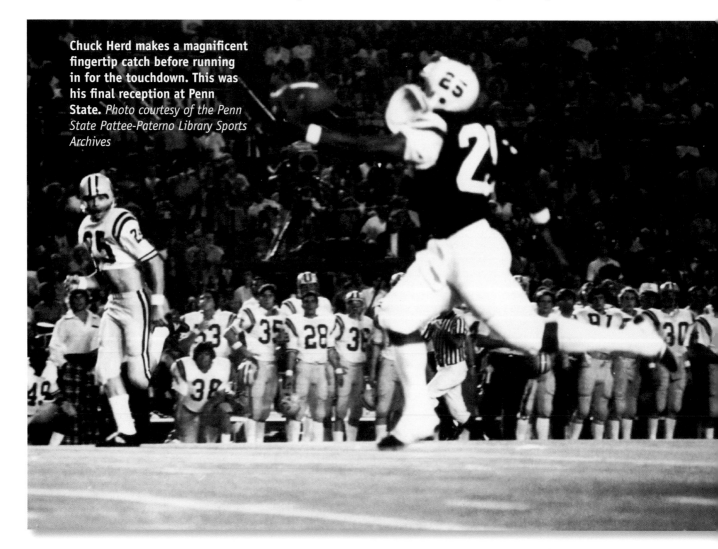

Chuck Herd makes a magnificent fingertip catch before running in for the touchdown. This was his final reception at Penn State. *Photo courtesy of the Penn State Pattee-Paterno Library Sports Archives*

It would be the only pass thrown to Herd in the game, just his 11th reception of the season, and the last one he'd ever make for Penn State.

The touchdown and Bahr's extra point put the Lions ahead to stay. Later in the quarter, Hayman's 35-yard punt return set up a short drive that climaxed with Cappelletti's one-yard vault for a touchdown. Bahr's kick attempt hit the goal post, but it wasn't needed in the end, as the second half turned into a conservative defensive game.

Cappelletti had been held to his lowest output of the year with 50 yards on 26 carries, but he didn't use his sprained ankle as an excuse. Neither did Paterno, who said Cappelletti "never really had any running room, and you'll have to blame the other team for that."

In the locker room, Paterno said "This was the best team I've ever coached. I don't know who is No. 1, but I think we have as much right to claim the top spot as anyone else. I have my own poll—the Paterno poll. The vote was unanimous—Penn State is No. 1."

And he can thank his Heisman Trophy winner and a little-known nimble-fingered wide receiver named Chuck Herd.

Game Details

Penn State 16 • Louisiana State 9

Penn State	3	13	0	0	**16**
LSU	7	0	2	0	9

Date: January 1, 1974

Team Records: Penn State 11–0, LSU 9–2

Scoring Plays:
LSU—Rogers three-yard run (Jackson PAT)
PSU—Bahr 44-yard FG
PSU—Herd 72-yard pass from Shuman (Bahr PAT)
PSU—Cappelletti one-yard run (kick failed)
LSU—Safety (Masella tackled in end zone)

Something for Joey

Outside of his coach, Joe Paterno, no one player is more synonymous with the Penn State football program than John Cappelletti.

That's what happens when you win the Heisman Trophy, make an emotional acceptance speech in honor of your dying 11-year-old brother, and then see your life's story turned into an inspirational book and movie years later.

Cappelletti's brother Joey had been fighting leukemia since he was three years old. And Joey was in the black-tie dinner audience that night in December 1973 when a tearful Cappelletti pointed him out and said, "If I can dedicate the trophy to [Joey] tonight and give him a couple days of happiness, this is worth everything...he has been a great inspiration to me." The standing ovation lasted for several minutes.

Joey passed away in April 1976, and a year later the TV movie and book *Something for Joey* were released. The book and movie continue to be used in school classrooms, and Cappelletti hears from many of the students on a weekly basis. "I'll get a package of letters from 30 or 40 kids from schools around the world," he said. "Reading the letters can get pretty emotional."

Cappelletti remains the only Penn State player ever to win college football's most prized award.

> **I** know my knee didn't touch the ground because I made a concerted effort not to touch my knee on the turf.
>
> **—GARY HAYMAN**

November 25, 1995

Mr. Clutch Does It Again

Bobby Engram's Touchdown Catch in Last Seconds Gives Lions Come-From-Behind Win

Bobby Engram was arguably the greatest Penn State player ever when the outcome of a game was on the line with the clock winding down, and someone had to make the big play. "He's the best I've ever had, and there have been very few like him," said coach Joe Paterno after the most remarkable pass reception of Engram's career beat Michigan State in a thrilling, come-from-behind, last-second win in 1995 at East Lansing.

Engram made many clutch receptions in his four years as a Nittany Lion wide receiver and several that were more meaningful than the one against Michigan State. In 1994 his 16-yard touchdown late in the fourth quarter that beat Michigan helped him win the first Biletnikoff Award as the country's outstanding receiver. But even though he didn't receive the Biletnikoff in 1995 or repeat as a first-team All-American, Engram was even more prolific in the clutch

when he was often seeing double and triple coverage and playing with a less experienced and occasionally erratic quarterback.

"The formula is simple for Penn State in 1995," wrote John Black in the Penn State *Football Letter*. "When the game is on the line, go to Bobby Engram." And that's precisely what happened in the last game of the season at East Lansing.

The game had postseason implications for New Year's Day with both teams battling for a third-place finish in the Big Ten and the conference's spot in the Outback Bowl. With a 7–3 record, the No. 14 Lions were a slight favorite over the unranked but surging Spartans, who had won their last five games to sport a 6–3–1 record.

There also was an interesting twist to the game. Michigan State's first-year coach, Nick Saban, had been hired when Penn State's offensive coordinator, Fran Ganter, had turned down the job after a very public courtship.

Bobby Engram makes a diving catch and falls over the goal line in the final seconds of the game to defeat MSU on November 25, 1995. *Photo courtesy of Joe Bodkin*

Bobby Engram

Bobby Engram, pictured here during the 1995 Rose Bowl, earned a reputation as being able to pull off huge plays during clutch, life-or-death moments of games.
Photo courtesy of Getty Images

Bobby Engram was more essential to the success of Penn State in 1995 than he was in 1994 when the undefeated No. 2 Nittany Lions won the Big Ten championship and Engram received the first Biletnikoff Award as the nation's outstanding receiver. Many of the players who made the 1994 team one of the greatest offenses in college football were gone in 1995, and without Engram's clutch receptions in three games, the Lions would have had a 5–6 season at best.

In midseason at Purdue, Engram caught a 49-yard bomb and a 14-yard pass in another late-fourth-quarter come-from-behind 80-yard rally and then drew two defenders as a decoy, enabling tailback Mike Archie to score on a screen pass and win the game 26–23. The next week at Iowa, Engram's diving 16-yard catch in the left corner of the end zone with 6:07 remaining broke a tight 27–27 deadlock, and minutes later Engram sealed the 41–27 victory with a 43-yard touchdown reception. Then came his dramatic last-second touchdown catch at Michigan State.

Had they lost those three games, Penn State would not have been anywhere near a postseason bowl game.

When he graduated, the 5'10", 185-pound Engram was the Lions' career leader in receptions, reception yardage, and touchdowns with 167 catches for 3,026 yards (an 18.1-yards-per-carry average) and 31 touchdowns. Fourteen years later, the greatest clutch player in Penn State's history was still catching those crucial passes in the NFL.

Michigan State had two weeks to prepare for the Thanksgiving weekend game, and Saban had devised a game plan with a defense to contain the Lions' running and pressure junior quarterback Wally Richardson. The Lions scored first but not until stopping the Spartans with an interception at the 4-yard line and then going 80 yards for a touchdown a minute into the second quarter. But Michigan State spurted ahead 10–7 by halftime and had a 17–10 lead early in the fourth quarter when, on a third-and-16, Engram caught a 53-yard touchdown pass to even the game again.

With 5:13 remaining, the Spartans broke the tie on a 28-yard field goal. They forced a punt with their third sack of the game, and as they took possession of the ball at 2:19 showing on the clock, their fans began celebrating. But with judicious use of timeouts and three defensive stops, Penn State made Michigan State punt. With the ball at their

Game Details

Penn State 24 • Michigan State 20

Penn State	0	7	3	14	**24**
Michigan State	0	10	0	10	**20**

Date: November 25, 1995
Team Records: Penn State 7–3,
Michigan State 6–3–1

Scoring Plays:

PSU—Milne one-yard run (Conway PAT)

MSU—Gardner 32-yard FG

MSU—Greene three-yard run (Gardner PAT)

PSU—Conway 42-yard FG

MSU—Greene 16-yard run (Gardner PAT)

PSU—Engram 53-yard pass from Richardson (Conway PAT)

MSU—Gardner 28-yard FG

PSU—Engram four-yard pass from Richardson (Conway PAT)

> **I** knew I was going to have to get in there—I sure wasn't going to coast in. All I saw was the goal line and green jerseys coming at me.
>
> —BOBBY ENGRAM

own 27 with 1:45 left and no timeouts, the outcome looked bleak for the Lions.

Richardson had looked edgy all day. He had hit on just 13 of 30 passes and thrown two interceptions. But Richardson transformed himself, taking the Lions downfield in 14 plays to the Spartans' 4-yard line with 34 seconds left. He completed 10 of 14 passes to five different receivers, using the sideline and spiking the ball for the second time after tight end Keith Olsommer's 13-yard catch brought the ball to the 4.

Disdaining a tying field goal, Paterno told Richardson to throw the same screen pass he had completed two plays before on his right side to halfback Mike Archie, only this time to throw it inside to Engram. "I told Wally, don't even look at Archie," Paterno said after the game. "Go to Bobby." With Michigan State defenders all around him, Engram took the quick pass at the 5-yard line, ducked between two Spartans about to crunch him, stumbled, and dove for the end zone as another defender roared up before fullback Brian Milne could get there to block. Engram stretched the ball past the goal line just as he was smothered by the tackler. There were eight seconds left on the clock, but the game was over.

It was the last regular-season reception of his career. Engram would catch four more in a 43–14, rain-soaked rout of Auburn in Tampa on January 1, marking the fifth straight year Penn State would play on New Year's Day (counting the January 2, 1995, Rose Bowl)—a streak that would reach eight before ending in 1999. Penn State's unofficial "Mr. Clutch" made it happen.

Heart-Stopping Tackles, Blocked Kicks, and Fumble Recoveries

October 18, 1969

Near Disaster in Syracuse

Blocked Field Goals and Fumble Recovery Help Avoid Devastating Upset

In reflecting back on Penn State's greatest football teams, the undefeated squads of 1968 and 1969 occupy a special and unique place in Nittany Lions history because they were the cornerstone for Joe Paterno's now-legendary coaching career.

Yet, if not for two defensive plays made by little-known junior defensive back George Landis in Syracuse's decrepit Archbold Stadium on a chilly October afternoon, it's unlikely the 1969 team would be held in such esteem. Without the two field-goal attempts that Landis blocked in the first half, Penn State would almost certainly have lost, and the 1969 Lions would never have reached their immortality.

What Landis unknowingly did was get into the head of Syracuse's own legendary coach, Ben Schwartzwalder, and cause him to make a rash decision that both he and Penn State's coach Joe Paterno later said was the turning point of the game.

Landis was a former offensive back who had practically no playing time until he became the surprise defensive starter when the season began. Then he became an integral part of the No. 5 team in the country with an undefeated streak of 23 games and an overwhelming favorite to defeat its longtime rival Syracuse in the fifth game of the season.

With a 3–1 record against weak opponents, Syracuse was not expected to be a serious threat to the Lions, but Paterno had cautioned his players about Schwartzwalder's skill in firing up his team whenever they played Penn State. Almost every game had ended in a controversy, and this one would too.

Syracuse took charge almost from the kickoff, and sophomore Greg Allen's long punt returns of Bob Parsons' booming kicks did the most damage. Early in the first quarter, Allen's 61-yard return put the Orangemen on the Lions' 27-yard line, but on fourth down Landis broke through to block a 38-yard field-goal attempt by George Jakowenko. Minutes later, a 32-yard return of an interception led to a five-play, 25-yard drive and a 7–0 Syracuse lead. As the first quarter was winding down, Allen did it again with a 65-yard return to the 8-yard line. Three plays later Syracuse had a stunning 14–0 lead with just 45 seconds gone in the second quarter.

Sophomore Franco Harris' running in this game at Syracuse helped the Lions come from behind to save the 1969 undefeated season with a narrow 15–14 victory.
Photo courtesy of the Penn State Pattee-Paterno Library Sports Archives

Syracuse Series

Penn State's rivalry with Syracuse in football was once extremely contemptuous. The first game on October 28, 1922, ended in a scoreless tie in New York's Polo Grounds, and the Lions didn't win until the sixth game of the series. From 1928 until 1940 the Lions won just three games, tied four, and lost six, including five straight defeats from 1931 to 1935. Penn State won nine straight starting in 1941, including Schwartzwalder's first year in 1949.

Nothing out of the ordinary occurred in 1950 and 1951, but after the 1953 game ended in a fist-swinging melee at the Syracuse sideline, the rivalry heated up.

Officiating became the prime focus of contention, including the 1958 game at Beaver Field where the Lions were penalized seven times, mostly for controversial interpretations of "illegal procedure" and "illegal shifts," in what Rip Engle said later was "the worst refereeing I've seen in 28 years."

Schwartzwalder extracted his revenge on Beaver Field the next season in what was the most significant game ever in the series. Syracuse won 20–18 and went on to win the national championship. But curiously, after the game both coaches were extremely gracious.

The teams stopped playing after 1990 with Penn State holding a 40–23–1 edge in the series and then resumed a two-game schedule in 2008–09, with the Lions winning the first game 55–13 at Syracuse.

George Landis' ability to block punts, like this one in a game at Beaver Stadium, was critical in the Nittany Lions' 15–14 win over underdog Syracuse in 1969. *Photo courtesy of the Penn State Pattee-Paterno Library Sports Archives*

Syracuse could have made it 17–0 later in the quarter when it reached the State 29-yard line, but Landis crashed through again to block another Jakowenko 38-yard field-goal try. With Parson again outkicking his coverage, Allen returned another punt 46 yards to the State 29, and as the first half neared the end, Syracuse had a fourth-and-a-long-1 at the 3-yard line. But Schwartzwalder passed up an easy field goal and called for a pitchout sweep to the right by Allen. Allen slipped, and the Lions ran out the clock.

"We tried two field goals earlier, and they were blocked," Schwartzwalder said after the game. "We only had a short distance to go."

Paterno said, "If they score it's all over. That was the turning point."

Paterno rallied his troops at halftime, and when Landis recovered a fumble at the Syracuse 12-yard line late in the third quarter it looked as if State had its first break. But the Lions were stopped on a fourth-and-3 at the 5, and as the fourth quarter began, things looked bleak for State.

Then Allen fumbled when hit by Dennis Onkotz, and Jack Ham recovered at the Syracuse 32. With State facing a fourth-and-6 at the 15, Syracuse was tagged with pass interference near the end zone, and Lydell Mitchell scored from the 4 on the next play. Paterno went for two points. Quarterback Chuck Burkhart passed to sophomore reserve fullback Franco Harris, but Harris was tackled at the 1. However, Syracuse was penalized again—for holding—and Harris then bolted around right end to make the score 14–8 as boos rained down from the partisan Syracuse crowd.

Syracuse almost bobbled the kickoff, and the State defense forced a short punt that rolled out at the Orange 39-yard line. On the second play, Burkhart faked to Charlie Pittman and gave the ball to Harris on a counter, and he ran 36 yards to tie the game. Mike Reitz's kick made it 15–14 with seven minutes left. It was all over when defensive back Neil Smith made his sixth interception of the year on the next series, and

the Lions were on the Orange 12-yard line when the game ended.

In a weekly luncheon of sportswriters in New York the following Monday, Schwartzwalder launched into a tirade blaming incompetent and biased officiating for his team's heartbreaking defeat. A livid Paterno suggested that Schwartzwalder should be sanctioned for unethical behavior.

Thus another Syracuse game ended in controversy, and the 1969 Nittany Lions went on to their special place in football history.

> They were pattern plays. It all depends on Jack Ham. If he does his job, I can block the kick. Ham knocks down the guy who's supposed to block me, and then I go around him.
>
> —GEORGE LANDIS

Game Details

Penn State 15 • Syracuse 14

Penn State	0	0	0	15	**15**
Syracuse	7	7	0	0	**14**

Date: October 18, 1969

Team Records: Penn State 4–0, Syracuse 3–1

Scoring Plays:

SYR—Newton one-yard run (Jakowenko PAT)

SYR—Zur six-yard run (Jakowenko PAT)

PSU—Mitchell four-yard run (Harris run)

PSU—Harris 36-yard run (Reitz PAT)

January 1, 1972

Redemption in the Cotton Bowl

Nittany Lions Come from Behind to Stuff the Texas Wishbone

When undefeated Penn State was upset at Tennessee in the last game of the 1971 season, everyone who had been perennially criticizing the Nittany Lions for their supposedly weak schedule of mostly inferior Eastern opponents gloated. "Imposter," one Tennessee newspaper had proclaimed, and that was *before* Tennessee's convincing 31–11 victory.

A Cotton Bowl game against Texas had already been locked up before the embarrassing loss in Knoxville, but now the Lions would be playing on New Year's Day for their reputation—and redemption. The critics laughed at the thought. Just three years earlier, many of its detractors had accused Penn State of ducking Texas in a national championship showdown game at the Cotton Bowl. This time they expected the Lions to get their comeuppance for that fateful decision.

The accepted theory was that Penn State would not be able to handle the Longhorns' potent Wishbone offense conceived in 1968 by Texas coach Darrell Royal. In the week leading up to the game, Lions coach Joe Paterno moaned about the problems his defense was having with the Wishbone in his closed practices. Some of his players admitted it was true, but they also were upset that Paterno was implying they weren't working hard enough.

The loss to Tennessee had dropped the Lions from No. 5 to No. 10 in the rankings, and the twice-beaten No. 12 Longhorns were a six-point favorite. The confident Texas fans expected the final score to be much higher, and the dreariness of the day—with a steady rain and temperatures hovering around 50 degrees—caused many who bought tickets to stay home and watch the game on TV.

But former president Lyndon Johnson, flashing the "Hook 'Em Horns" sign for the cameras, was among the announced crowd of 72,000 as Texas dominated the first quarter with long drives to the State 30- and 1-yard lines. However, the Lions held the Longhorns to a 29-yard field goal and then forced a fumble at the Texas 20 early in the second quarter that led to a 21-yard tying field goal. Texas stayed on the attack throughout the quarter, missing a long field goal, but State's defense was getting into a

Jim Laslavic tackles Eddie Phillips in Penn State's victory over Texas in the 1972 Cotton Bowl. *Photo courtesy of Penn State Athletic Communications*

rhythm. Neither team could get an edge until a Longhorns interception with about 30 seconds left in the half gave them the ball at their own 40, and on the last play of the half they kicked a 40-yard field goal.

With Texas getting the second-half kickoff, the partisan crowd and the Texas beat writers in the press box anticipated a rout in the second half. They got one, but not what they had expected. As Lions co-captain and All-American offensive tackle Dave Joyner told Paterno in the locker room, "We got 'em where we want 'em."

It started moments after the kickoff with three plays that changed the game. On the Longhorns' first possession, quarterback Eddie Phillips fumbled the wet ball at midfield. Defensive end Jim Laslavic inadvertently kicked it downfield, and All-American linebacker and co-captain Chuck Zapiec recovered at the Texas 41. Lydell Mitchell ran 20 yards, and on second-and-8, quarterback John Hufnagel

found converted tight end Bob Parsons wide open behind the Texas safety for a pass completion to the 1-yard line. Mitchell banged over for the touchdown, and Penn State's sudden 10–6 lead seemed to paralyze the Longhorns.

The Lions forced a punt after the kickoff, and on second down at the State 35, split end John Skarzynski ran past the safety, took Hufnagel's pass at about the 50, and ran into the end zone. Al Vitiello's PAT made it 17–6 with just about six and a half minutes gone in the second half, but the game was virtually over from that point. State's defense shut down the vaunted Texas Wishbone, and the Lions' offense controlled the ball for nearly 13 minutes of the fourth quarter. Penn State won handily, 30–6, holding the Wishbone to a net 242 yards and preventing high-scoring Texas from getting a touchdown for the first time in 80 games.

Linebacker Gary Gray (No. 30), defensive tackle Frank Ahrenhold (No. 79), linebacker Charlie Zapiec (No. 60), and defensive end Jim Laslavic (No. 47) gang tackle a Texas runner in the Cotton Bowl on January 1, 1972. *Photo courtesy of the Penn State Pattee-Paterno Library Sports Archives*

Changing Positions

Joe Paterno is well known for switching players from one position to another for the overall benefit of the team. Some of the moves seem capricious at first, but they usually turn out best for Penn State and the player s involved. The 1971 team exemplified the validity of the Paterno philosophy.

Four of the key players in the 1972 Cotton Bowl started out in different positions. Charlie Zapiec had been a starting offensive guard on the undefeated 1968–69 teams and moved to inside linebacker in 1970. He played in one game before an appendectomy sidelined him for the year, but in 1971 Zapiec became an All-American at linebacker and then had a long career in the Canadian Football League.

Jim Laslavic was a double switcher. He was a backup linebacker in 1970, moved to defense in 1971, and was back at linebacker the next season. Laslavic never made All-American, but he was a starting linebacker in the NFL for nearly 10 years.

Bob Parsons had been the backup quarterback as a sophomore and junior as well as the team's punter. Paterno moved him to tight end in his senior year and he made the All-East team. Parsons spent 11 years with the Chicago Bears as a tight end and punter.

Then there was a starting defensive back on that Cotton Bowl team, a sophomore named John Cappelletti. The next year Cappelletti was the Lions' starting tailback and in 1973 won the Heisman Trophy.

In the eyes of both coaches and the writers in the press box, the key plays of the game were Zapiec's fumble recovery and Hufnagel's passes to Parson and Skarzynski. But the true reason for the final outcome was the Penn State defense, playing out of a basic 5-3-3 formation but trained to stunt consistently, contain the inside and outside, and gang tackle.

"I don't think we've ever had a game that we had to win more than this one," Paterno said in the locker room. "There was so much that had been done that was ready to go down the drain if Texas had beaten us." Years later, Paterno called the victory "one of the greatest victories in Penn State history.

Redemption!

> They were in a two-deep coverage, and I guess the safety made a mistake. When Huf threw the ball I was so far open I knew we had a touchdown. My grandmother could have made the play.
>
> —JOHN SKARZYNSKI

Game Details

Penn State 30 • Texas 6

Penn State	0	3	17	10	**30**
Texas	3	3	0	0	**6**

Date: January 1, 1972

Team Records: Penn State 10–1, Texas 8–2

Scoring Plays:

TEX—Valek 29-yard FG

PSU—Vitiello 21-yard FG

TEX—Valek 40-yard FG

PSU—Mitchell one-yard run (Vitiello PAT)

PSU—Skarzynski 65-yard pass from Hufnagel (Vitiello PAT)

PSU—37-yard FG

PSU—Vitiello 22-yard FG

PSU—Hufnagel four-yard run (Vitiello PAT)

November 15, 1986

Bob and Ray Save the Day

Last-Minute Goal-Line Stand at Notre Dame Saves Championship Season

The glisten off the hallowed Golden Dome that overshadows Notre Dame Stadium seemed dimmer in the early 1980s when the Irish football team plummeted into mediocrity. But on a cold late-November afternoon in 1986, the magic echoes of past glory came alive and almost ruined Penn State's national championship season.

One week before, the Nittany Lions had barely escaped an upset tie with Maryland at home that would not only have eliminated them from the national championship but also dropped them to No. 3 in the polls behind Miami and Michigan. Now the Lions were in South Bend to play a resurging Notre Dame team that had won three straight after starting the season at 1–4 under new coach Lou Holtz.

Holtz was the perfect man to wake up the echoes against Penn State, for he had twice upset the Lions as coach at North Carolina State from 1972 to 1975. And it must have been more than happenstance that Notre Dame chose this November weekend to honor its undefeated team of 1966 that shared the national championship with Michigan State after their historic controversial 10–10 tie.

The oddsmakers must have suspected something, too, because with nine straight victories, Penn State was just a four-and-a-half-point favorite, and Notre Dame showed why on its first possession. As vice president George Bush and the sellout throng of 59,075 watched, Notre Dame forced a punt after kicking off to Penn State and drove to the Lions' 21-yard line.

Suddenly, everything changed. Lions tackle Bob White stripped the ball from quarterback Steve Beuerlein as he was being tackled by end Don Graham, and linebacker Pete Giftopoulos recovered at the 18. Eleven plays later Penn State was in front 7–0 with 5:54 left in the first quarter. Notre Dame appeared to strike back on the ensuing kickoff when Tim Brown ran 97 yards for a touchdown, but it was called back by a clipping penalty.

The Irish dominated the rest of the half, eventually controlling the ball for a total of 18 minutes. But Penn State's big-play defense came through when it counted, twice stopping Notre Dame deep in Lions territory and forcing the Irish to kick field goals. Then, with Notre Dame trying to run out the clock before halftime, linebacker Shane Conlan forced another Beuerlein fumble, tackle Pete Curkendall recovered at the Notre

Dame 23, and with 1:03 left, Massimo Manca's 19-yard field goal gave the outplayed Lions a 10–6 halftime lead.

The Irish came out swinging, taking the second-half kickoff and going 92 yards in six plays to go ahead on Beuerlein's 14-yard pass to Brown. Just as quickly, the momentum shifted. Before the end of the third quarter, the Lions scored on a six-play, 82-yard drive, then scored again 3:11 into the fourth quarter on a 56-yard, nine-play march that gave them a 24–13 lead.

But Notre Dame struck back again, going 64 yards for a touchdown, but a pass for two failed. The score remained 24–19 as the teams traded possessions until the Irish had

Bob White was skilled at harassing quarterbacks, such as in this game against Rutgers, and his two game-changing plays in the 1986 Notre Dame game were vital in Penn State's 24–19 victory. *Photo courtesy of Penn State Athletic Communications*

the ball again at their own 20-yard line with 2:29 remaining. In 53 seconds and five straight pass completions, Beuerlein had the Irish at the 6-yard line with a first-and-goal and 1:28 on the clock.

"It's six yards," safety Ray Isom said later. "You let 'em in, the season is over."

On the first play, Notre Dame called a two-tight-end option pass to Brown. The play was designed to take advantage of State's goal-line defense, leaving Isom to cover Brown alone on the Irish left flat with a tight end to block Isom. But the second tight end never entered the game, and Isom smacked Notre Dame's future Heisman Trophy winner for a three-yard loss.

After an Irish timeout, Beuerlein went back to pass and was sacked by Bob White, who had faked the Irish tackle by lining up to the outside but cut inside instead to slam Beuerlein down for a nine-yard loss. "The sack was the play of the game," Holtz said later.

Disrupting opposing team plays, as shown here in a game against Temple, was safety Ray Isom's forte, and no play was bigger than his crucial first-down tackle in the 1986 Notre Dame game. *Photo courtesy of Penn State Athletic Communications*

Other 1986 Game Changers

Without Penn State's crucial goal-line stand against Notre Dame, the Nittany Lions would never have played for the national championship in the 1987 Fiesta Bowl. But the thrilling win over the Irish would not have been as meaningful if Penn State had not made other great plays in two earlier games that season.

In the fifth game of the year, a heavily underdog Cincinnati team led the undefeated Lions 17–14 with about six minutes left in the game and a third-and-1 at the State 49-yard line. Cincinnati's Reggie Taylor tried to slash up the middle but was thrown for a one-yard loss by tackle Pete Curkendall. Moments afterward, Penn State had a third-and-2 at its own 33,

when little-used sophomore tailback Blair Thomas took a short pass from John Shaffer and ran to the Cincy 35 for a first down. Four plays later Penn State scored and went on to win 23–17.

A week before the Notre Dame game, the Lions almost blew a 17–9 lead with 1:04 left against Maryland. The Terps went 73 yards and passed for a 27-yard touchdown with 14 seconds remaining on a fourth-and-7. But sophomore linebacker Keith Karpinski forced Maryland's quarterback to hurry his two-point passing attempt, and safety Duffy Cobbs knocked the ball down at the 1, preserving the 17–15 win.

Notre Dame called its last timeout with 52 seconds left. Then Beuerlein almost made the play of the game on third down when he found tight end Joe Williams wide open in the end zone. In rushed backup cornerback Gary Wilkerson, who belted Williams, and the ball bounced off his fingertips.

With 47 seconds remaining, State went into a prevent defense. Notre Dame sent three receivers into the end zone, but they were covered, and Beuerlein desperately flipped the ball off five yards to tailback Mark Green near the right sideline. Green was boxed in by Shane Conlan and Pete Giftopoulos, and as he caught the ball he slipped and his knee touched the ground.

The Irish luck had run out.

> **W**e were in our short-yardage, goal-line defense. I knew I was out there by myself. I had to make the tackle or the season was over.
>
> —RAY ISOM

Game Details

Penn State 24 • Notre Dame 19

Penn State	7	3	7	7	**24**
Notre Dame	0	6	7	6	**19**

Date: November 15, 1986

Team Records: Penn State 9–0, Notre Dame 4–4

Scoring Plays:

PSU—Smith one-yard run (Manca PAT)

NDU—Carney 20-yard FG

NDU—Carney 38-yard FG

PSU—Manca 19-yard FG

NDU—Brown 14-yard pass from Beuerlein (Carney PAT)

PSU—Roundtree 37-yard pass from Shaffer (Manca PAT)

PSU—Shaffer one-yard run (Manca PAT)

NDU—Brown eight-yard pass from Beuerlein (pass failed)

January 1, 1970

The Swarming Defense That Beat Every Opponent but a President

Dominating Defense Caps Second Straight Perfect Season

The 1969 season was the most controversial ever for Penn State football because the president of the United States injected himself into the determination of the No. 1 team, and the Nittany Lions unfortunately passed up a chance to play for the national championship on New Year's Day. The team is now celebrated as one of the greatest in school history with a defense that was one of the best ever in college football.

As the 1969 Lions were advancing through what eventually would be a 31-game undefeated streak, they made a regrettable but complicated decision that would haunt the team forever. In that era, bowl matchups were set before the end of regular-season games. With seemingly no chance at a national championship game and a disdain for the racist practices in the Deep South and Southwest,

the team voted to return to the Orange Bowl instead of playing the Southwest Conference champion in Dallas.

It all blew up in their face when Michigan upset No. 1 Ohio State, and Texas defeated Arkansas with president Richard Nixon in attendance in Austin to award what he declared was the "national championship" to the winning team. Nixon's political ploy to appeal to Southern voters ignited a firestorm that continues to smolder to this day, and No. 2 Penn State is still castigated for avoiding a showdown Cotton Bowl game against Texas.

Throughout the decades, Penn State has been criticized, fairly or not, for its schedule. That was the foundation for Big 12 champion Missouri to be a three-point favorite. The Tigers averaged 450 yards and 36 points per game and never scored less than 17 points in rolling to a 9–1 record. Skeptics were convinced State's defense was overrated, despite allowing just 87 points in 10 victories,

Quarterback Chuck Burkhart (No. 22) passes to Lydell Mitchell (No. 23) for the first-quarter touchdown in the Orange Bowl against Missouri on January 1, 1970. *Photo courtesy of AP Images*

and could not handle Missouri's power. They soon found out differently.

Paterno had closed his pregame practices and had tinkered with his defense, adding zone coverage to the basic man-to-man and spicing up his passing attack with new plays. Missouri was surprised on the first play of the game when Penn State passed from a shotgun formation. Midway through the quarter, the Lions went from the PSU 20 to the Tigers 16 before bogging down and getting a 29-yard field goal by Mike Reitz.

Missouri fumbled the ensuing kickoff, and after the Lions recovered at the Missouri 28, Paterno sent in the special pass play he had designed just for this game. Sophomore reserve tailback Lydell Mitchell drifted toward the left sideline, caught Chuck Burkhart's throw on the 24, and ran for the touchdown. Reitz's kick made it 10–0 with

1:56 left in the quarter, and although no one knew it at the time, those 10 points would win the game.

For the rest of the night, Penn State's defense owned the stadium. With just a four-man rush and a rare blitz, the swarming defense intercepted an Orange Bowl–record seven passes and recovered two fumbles—both by end John Ebersole—and stopped Missouri a half-dozen times in scoring territory. Missouri's best drive came near the end of the first half when it went from its own 8-yard line to State's 7 before a sack by All-American tackle Mike Reid and an incomplete pass forced the Tigers to settle for their only points of the night on a 33-yard field goal.

Actually the Lions missed several opportunities to score in the second half, and the one near the end of the third quarter almost cost them the game. With the help of a 56-yard bomb by Burkhart, the Lions went 66 yards to the Tigers' 7 before attempting a fourth-down field goal from the 10. Reitz's kick went off the side of his foot, low

Lydell Mitchell scores the only touchdown in Penn State's victory over Missouri in the 1970 Orange Bowl to secure a perfect season for the Nittany Lions. *Photo courtesy of the Penn State Pattee-Paterno Library Sports Archives*

George Landis

George Landis was probably the least-known player on what was arguably Penn State's best-ever defensive team in 1969. Forty years later he still is.

The defense was loaded with four first-team All-Americans—Jack Ham, Dennis Onkotz, Neal Smith, and Mike Reid, who won the Maxwell Award in 1969.

And then there was Landis. As a sophomore in 1968, he started out as a little-used reserve running back and was switched to defensive halfback, where he saw enough playing time to earn a letter. Landis passed up spring drills to be the starting catcher on the baseball team, and when the 1969 preseason practice started he was listed as a third-team halfback.

But Landis developed so well in the preseason that Joe Paterno made him a starter. In the second game of the season against Colorado, Landis had two interceptions. Three weeks later at Syracuse, Landis blocked two field-goal attempts that helped Penn State avoid a devastating defeat in a come-from-behind 15–14 victory. Then came his goal-line interception that clinched the Orange Bowl win over Missouri.

Ham, Onkotz, and Reid were eventually enshrined in the College Football Hall of Fame, but Landis has been all but forgotten—until now.

and wide. "A field goal wins it right there," Paterno mused later.

But the game was still on the line in the last two minutes when Missouri's backup quarterback Chuck Roper threw two quick passes that moved the Tigers from the Missouri 42 to State's 14 with 1:42 remaining. State's defense forced two incomplete passes, and then came the play of the game.

Junior halfback George Landis, perhaps the least-known player on the defense, who had helped avoid an upset at Syracuse that year, stepped in front of Roper's third-down pass at the 2-yard line and ran 55 yards before being brought down. Not only was that Landis' second interception of the night, but it set the Orange Bowl record. The game, the season, and the 1969 team's legacy was sealed. Take that, Mr. President!

Game Details

Penn State 10 • Missouri 3

Penn State	10	0	0	0	**10**
Missouri	0	3	0	0	**3**

Date: January 1, 1970
Team Records: Penn State 10–0, Missouri 9–1

Scoring Plays:
PSU—Reitz 29-yard FG
PSU—Mitchell 28-yard pass from Burkhart (Reitz PAT)
MIS—Brown 33-yard FG

I didn't know until noon I was going to play [because of my foot injury]. I'm just thanking God I could play...I didn't know [the interception] was a record, but I knew it was a pretty good average.
—GEORGE LANDIS

October 8, 2005

Hali Strips the Buckeyes

Lions Take Big Ten Lead as Tamba Hali Forces Late Fumble to Upset Ohio State

The image of defensive end Tamba Hali stripping the ball away from Buckeyes quarterback Troy Smith late in the fourth quarter of this game and belting him upside down into the air is forever frozen in the annals of Nittany Lions football.

It was the midway point of the season, and the Lions had just broken into the top 25 at No. 16 after a 44–14 pounding of Minnesota, while once-beaten Ohio State was No. 6 and slight three-point favorites. This game was expected to be the true test for a surprising Penn State team still being doubted by fans and the media after successive 3–9 and 4–7 losing seasons.

The weeklong pregame atmosphere matched the excitement and hysteria of any game ever played at Beaver Stadium. Students camped out for days in 100 tents at a new site near their entrance gate that they dubbed "Paternoville," ticket prices soared to

a premium, and ESPN was on hand for three days originating shows and reporting on the hype.

By the time of the scheduled 7:45 PM kickoff, the rain that had fallen for almost two days had tapered off. And the jacked-up thousands of fans, most of them wearing white for what was officially called "a whiteout," waited to see if their Nittany Lions could beat a top 10 team for the first time since 1999.

With both teams among the nation's best in total defense plus a wet and slippery grass field, a defensive clash was expected, and it was delivered. A shanked punt on the Lions' first possession gave the Buckeyes the ball at their 43-yard line, and they went 44 yards in 12 plays before settling for a 30-yard field goal. But at 4:40 of the second quarter, Penn State took a 7–3 lead after a nine-play, 74-yard march, highlighted by a 16-yard scramble by quarterback Michael Robinson, Tony Hunt's three-yard run on a fourth-and-1 at the

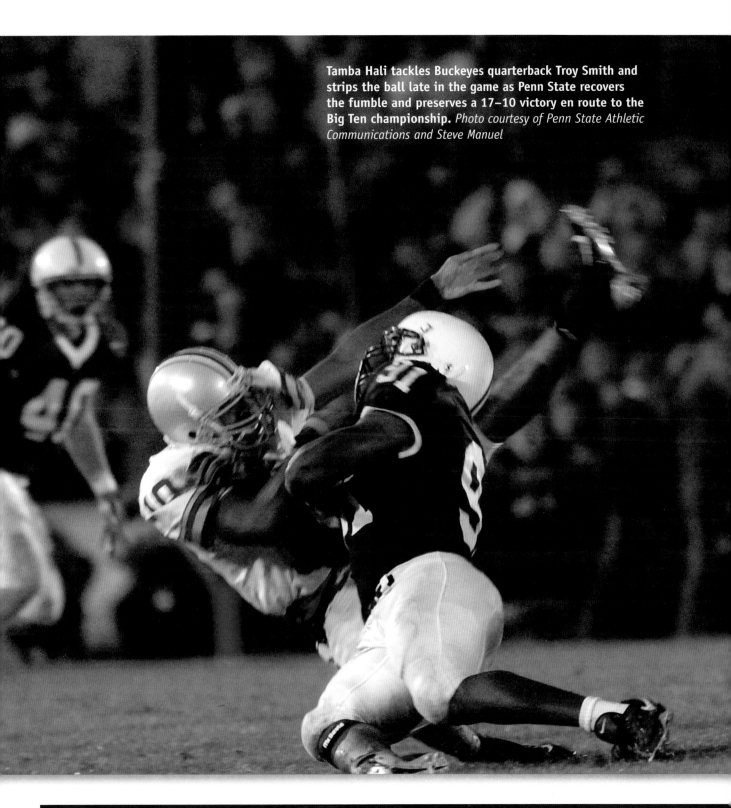

Tamba Hali tackles Buckeyes quarterback Troy Smith and strips the ball late in the game as Penn State recovers the fumble and preserves a 17–10 victory en route to the Big Ten championship. *Photo courtesy of Penn State Athletic Communications and Steve Manuel*

OSU 35, and true freshman Derrick Williams' 13-yard touchdown on a pitchout from Robinson.

Two and a half minutes later, Penn State's lead was 14–3 when safety Calvin Lowry's 36-yard interception return to the OSU 2-yard line set up Robinson's one-yard touchdown. With the crowd noise at an increasing decibel level, the Lions seemed to be in control. "You could feel a tingle up your spine," Robinson remembered later. But with about eight minutes left in the half, Ohio State methodically drove 81 yards in 14 plays and scored with 33 seconds remaining.

On the Lions' first possession of the third quarter, they went 45 yards in 10 plays and stretched their lead to 17–10 on true freshman Kevin Kelly's 41-yard field goal. Then OSU barely missed a 50-yard field goal, but from that point the defenses took over with neither team moving too far past midfield.

As the clock wound down in the fourth quarter, the uproarious crowd was on its feet as tackle Jay Alford slammed Smith to the turf to end one Buckeyes possession, and linebacker Paul Posluszny ran Smith down behind the line of scrimmage to end another. With 3:37 remaining, a punt by Jeremy Kapinos backed Ohio State to its own 11-yard line, and in the next few moments the stadium literally shook because of the stomping and yelling of the Lions fans.

But suddenly, Ohio State was at the Penn State 45 after Smith's 26-yard pass to Ted Ginn and his 21-yard pass to Santonio Holmes. The clock showed 1:28 when Smith took the snap. Hali blasted past a blocker on OSU's left side and was on top of the quarterback before he knew it. In one swift move, Hali smashed Smith into the air as he stripped the ball away from Smith's right hand. Tackle Scott Paxson jumped on the ball, and the crowd erupted in what can only be described as pandemonium. "I saw the ball on the ground, and my eyes lit up," Paxson said later.

The celebration went on for hours in the damp stadium parking lots and the bars and taverns of State College. "In all the years I have been here, I have never seen more spontaneous enthusiasm," coach Joe Paterno said after the game.

With the victory, Penn State took the lead for the Big Ten championship, and but for a heartbreaking two-point, controversial loss the next week at Michigan on the last play of the game, the Cinderella Lions might have played for the BCS national championship. They went on to beat Florida State in triple overtime at the Orange Bowl and finished with their highest final ranking in the polls in 11 years at No. 3. Tamba Hali's sack still lives in all those memories.

> **I** was picking up speed, and I could see that he wasn't looking. I hit him, and I saw the ball come out. Then I saw Paxson pick it up. I was glad because I was kind of tired.
>
> —TAMBA HALI

Game Details

Penn State 17 • Ohio State 10

Ohio State	3	7	0	0	**10**
Penn State	0	14	3	0	**17**

Date: October 8, 2005

Team Records: Penn State 5–0, Ohio State 3–1

Scoring Plays:

OSU—Huston 30-yard FG
PSU—Williams 13-yard run (Kelly PAT)
PSU—Robinson one-yard run (Kelly PAT)
OSU—Smith 10-yard run (Huston PAT)
PSU—Kelly 41-yard FG

An Old Tradition—Fight Songs

The student camping tentsite dubbed "Paternoville" is a new Penn State tradition, but the band music played at every home game goes back almost 100 years.

Two of the songs, "The Nittany Lion" and "Fight On State," are still featured as part of the flashy pregame festivities when Penn State's Blue Band enters Beaver Stadium and marches down the field in the "Floating Lion" formation. A third song, "Victory," also is played during the game.

Jimmy Leyden wrote both "Victory" and "The Nittany Lion." He was a sophomore in 1913 when he wrote "Victory." Then, while working in New York in the summer of 1919, Leyden wrote "The Nittany Lion," now better known by its opening words, "Hail to the Lion, Loyal and True." Leyden introduced both songs at football games, standing in the middle of the field and singing the words through a large megaphone with a cornet accompanying him.

"Fight on State" was written in 1935 by Joseph Saunders, a 1915 graduate then living in Atlantic City. The song was originally given to the freshman class to sing as its song, but it was so catchy that it was soon adopted by the entire student body and Blue Band.

And that's how traditions are made.

During days leading up to particularly important games, fans camp out in a tent village known as Paternoville. *Photo courtesy of Penn State Athletic Communications and Steve Manuel*

November 11, 1967

The Goal-Line Stand

Last-Minute Fourth-Down Tackle Surprises North Carolina State

Coach Joe Paterno has called the fourth-down goal-line stand against North Carolina State at Beaver Stadium in 1967 "one of the greatest plays in Penn State history." It was the play that not only beat the No. 3 team in the nation but is also the one that first thrust Paterno into national prominence.

Yet, if Paterno had persisted in using the defensive scheme he actually wanted to on that play, his legendary career might have been radically different.

This was just his 18th game as head coach, and although his Nittany Lions finally had a winning record that season at 5–2, memories of his mediocre 5–5 debut the previous year were still fresh. After an opening-game defeat at Navy, Paterno had made a drastic change in the first quarter of the next game at Miami by inserting more than a half-dozen previously untested sophomores into the defensive lineup, and their performance helped upset the Hurricanes 17–8.

But Penn State was nowhere near the top 10, while the veteran NC State team with 17 seniors in its starting offense and defense was on the verge of its first undefeated season in 57 years and a spot in the Sugar Bowl. Surprisingly, the Lions were a two-point favorite.

There also was a twist to the game. The head coach at NC State was Earle Edwards, a one-time player and longtime assistant coach at Penn State, and his staff included two other former Nittany Lions players. Paterno admitted the Edwards connection gave him an extra incentive to win this game.

Paterno decided to surprise the visitors with the shotgun formation that switched tight end Ted Kwalick into the slot on the left side. It paid off immediately. The Lions drove downfield in five plays from their 47-yard line and scored when Kwalick snared an overthrown pass from Tom Sherman for an 18-yard touchdown just three and a half minutes into the game (see p. 39).

NC State went to the air to try and tie the game, and three minutes later one of Paterno's new sophomore starters, linebacker Dennis Onkotz, intercepted and ran down the sideline 67 yards for a touchdown. "That was the big play of the game," Paterno said later in the locker room. "It's what gave us the momentum to win." This time Sherman's extra-point kick failed.

Both teams missed scoring opportunities as the game progressed on that cloudy but windy and unseasonably mild afternoon. Twice in the second half, NC State had to settle for field goals inside the PSU 10, and it lost another opportunity on an end zone interception.

Then, with 4:47 remaining in the game, the Wolfpack took over at its 32-yard line following a punt and in 11-plays drove to a first-and-goal just inside the Penn State 10 with 1:41 on the clock and all three timeouts.

NC State's star tailback Tony Barchuk already had gained 92 yards on 27 carries, and on first down he picked up one more. Then the Wolfpack surprised the Lions by sending fullback Bobby Hall up the middle for six. After a timeout, Hull moved the ball to the 1, and with 44 seconds left, North Carolina State called its second timeout.

Wolfpack quarterback Jim Donnan went to the sideline and told Edwards the players wanted a play that had already been successful—a fake to the fullback and handoff to the tailback Barchuk going over the right tackle. Edwards thought about a pitchout but reluctantly gave the go-ahead. Across the field Paterno was having a similar discussion with defensive back Tim Montgomery and defensive coordinator Jim O'Hora. Paterno thought NC State would fake to the fullback and go outside with the tailback. Montgomery said he believed the tailback would go inside after the fake. Paterno was doubtful but told O'Hora and Montgomery to defend inside.

Donnan faked to Hall and handed off to Barchuk. Tackle Mike McBath submarined the hole and grabbed Barchuk's leg as Onkotz hit him high and fellow sophomore linebacker Jim Kates hit him low, and they slammed the

Mike McBath (No. 73), Dennis Onkotz (No. 35), and Jim Kates (No. 55) stop North Carolina State's Tony Barchuck on this fourth-and-goal from the 1-yard line to upset North Carolina State 13–8 in 1967. *Photo courtesy of the Penn State All-Sports Museum*

Fans celebrate in the end zone after Penn State upsets North Carolina State in the 1967 game that propelled coach Joe Paterno into the national spotlight for the first time. *Photo courtesy of the Penn State All-Sports Museum*

The Alumni Coaches

Earle Edwards was handpicked to succeed Bob Higgins as Penn State's head coach in 1949, but when he was passed over, he left the Nittany Lions and eventually created his own legendary career at North Carolina State.

Edwards had been a starting end for Penn State from 1928 to 1930. He returned in 1936 and joined two other former players, Joe Bedenk and Al Michaels, on Higgins' coaching staff. Through the years, Edwards became Higgins' closest confidante.

When Higgins suddenly announced his retirement in March 1949 because of health reasons, he told the administration Edwards should succeed him. Bedenk didn't want to apply for the job, but friends in the athletic department and some ex-teammates pulled some strings behind the scene and Bedenk was named head coach instead of Edwards. After spring practice, the disappointed Edwards left to be an assistant at Michigan State.

In 1954 Edwards became the head coach at North Carolina State and hired another former Penn State player, Bill Smaltz, then the head coach at Juniata. Michaels joined them two years later, and they were still there when Edwards retired after the 1970 season and Michaels succeeded him. The alumni coaches lost three games against their alma mater in 1956, 1967, and 1969.

tailback to the ground. The crowd was on its feet screaming, but the game wasn't over.

The Lions ran three plays as time wound down between NC State timeouts before the punter took a safety with two seconds left. After punting from the 20, the Lions stopped the Wolfpack's last play at the Lions' 39.

"I should have called another play," Edwards said in the visitors' locker room. In the other locker room, Paterno gave full credit to Montgomery. "I sure as hell would have screwed it up," Paterno said.

A week later, the Lions accepted an invitation to the Gator Bowl, and Paterno's legendary career was on its way.

> **T**im Montgomery was really the guy who stopped them by calling the inside defense.
>
> **—JOE PATERNO**

Game Details

Penn State 13 • North Carolina State 8

NC State	0	0	6	2	**8**
Penn State	13	0	0	0	**13**

Date: November 11, 1967

Team Records: Penn State 5–2,
North Carolina State 8–0

Scoring Plays:

PSU—Kwalick 18-yard pass from Sherman (Sherman PAT)

PSU—Onkotz 67-yard interception (kick failed)

NCS—Warren 23-yard FG

NCS—Warren 26-yard FG

NCS—Safety (Cherry ran out of end zone)

October 25, 2008

Rubin's Pryor Sandwich

Fumble Sparks Late Rally for First-Ever Big Ten Win at the Horseshoe

Mark Rubin's jarring tackle that stripped the ball from Ohio State's gifted freshman quarterback Tyrell Pryor late in the game at Columbus in the ninth week of the season was the single-most-important play in Penn State's surprising run to the Big Ten championship and Rose Bowl in 2008. The play was so crucial to the team's successful 11–2 record and No. 8 ranking in the final polls that it was one of 14 plays in the college season selected by ESPN for its "Pontiac Game-Changing Performance."

The Nittany Lions had not beaten the Buckeyes in their own stadium since entering the Big Ten in 1993, and for the first time, Penn State was the favorite, by two and a half points.

Penn State's 2008 team was almost overlooked in the preseason and was ranked No. 22 in both major polls. With many veterans from the last two BCS National Championship Games, the Buckeyes were rated at No. 2 or No. 3.

By game night, Penn State had leaped to No. 3 after eight wins, including an overwhelming 48–7 rout of Wisconsin in Madison two weeks earlier. And just the week before, the Lions defeated Michigan for the first time in 10 games, 46–17, at Beaver Stadium. Meanwhile, Ohio State was just regaining respect after

I just tried to squeeze tight and make a play. I just wanted to make a sure tackle. I knew it was third-and-short, so I didn't want to let him get the first down. I just tried to square up and push him back. I'm not going to lie, I just happened to punch it out.

—MARK RUBIN

In one of college football's game-changing plays of 2008, Mark Rubin strips the ball from Buckeyes quarterback Tyrell Pryor in a nationally televised night game at Columbus. *Photo courtesy of* Blue White Illustrated *and Mark Selders*

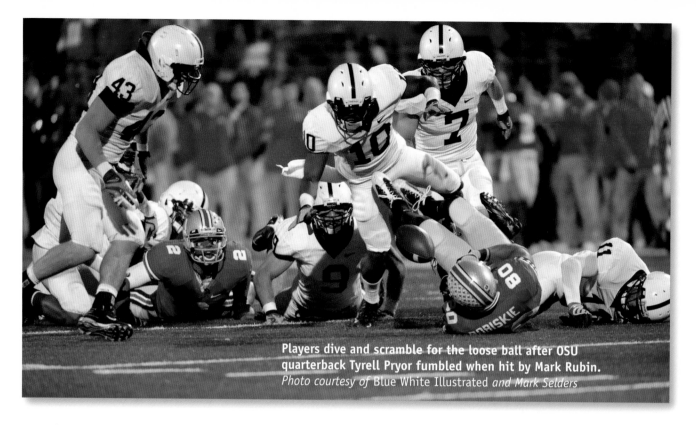

Players dive and scramble for the loose ball after OSU quarterback Tyrell Pryor fumbled when hit by Mark Rubin. *Photo courtesy of* Blue White Illustrated *and Mark Selders*

an embarrassing 35–3 loss at Southern California in week three and, with a 7–1 record, was now ranked No. 10.

Junior Daryll Clark had seen little playing time for two seasons, but with the help of a fleet of veteran receivers, he was the linchpin for the Lions' success with his passing, running, and leadership. Coach Jim Tressel had benched his senior quarterback after the debacle at USC and inserted Pryor, who had been the nation's No. 1 high school recruit out of Jeannette, Pennsylvania, and had chosen OSU over Penn State after a high-profile recruiting battle.

But in the end, the game came down to defense. It was the first night game at Ohio Stadium in three years, and a record crowd of 105,711 sitting in the damp cold saw the teams trade field goals in the first half and the Buckeyes take a 6–3 lead with another field goal with 3:19 left in the third quarter.

After the kickoff, the Lions reached OSU's 28-yard line but missed a 45-yard field goal, and the Buckeyes took over with 11:19 remaining in the fourth quarter. In five plays the Buckeyes were at the Lions' 41 with a third-and-1. Tressel

called for a quarterback sneak, but as Pryor took the snap he thought he saw an opening to his right and bounced that way.

The Lions had expected a sneak and called a safety blitz. In one motion Rubin hit Pryor and with his left hand stripped the ball out of Pryor's loose grip. OSU's star tailback Beanie Wells dove for it, but he was hit by linebacker Tyrell Sales, who pushed the ball out of reach. Buckeyes receiver Brian Robiskie reached for the ball just as he was hit by cornerback Tony Davis, and the ball squirmed away toward sophomore linebacker Navorro Bowman, who grabbed it and covered it up with his body at the 38-yard line.

The crowd was surprised to see backup Lions quarterback Pat Devlin trot out instead of Clark. It was later revealed that Clark had suffered a concussion during the last Lions drive, but it wasn't noticed at first. With 10:38 left, the game was in the hands of a highly touted redshirt sophomore.

After a nine-yard run by Evan Royster on the first play, a pass-interference penalty moved Penn State to the 14.

Paterno in the Press Box

The familiar, iconic scene of Joe Paterno wearing his black football shoes, white socks, and high-cuffed trousers while he paced the sideline at Penn State football games was missing in 2008. A painful injury to his right leg forced him to coach most of the season from the press box, and he was not particularly happy about it.

"You like to be on the field," Paterno said. "You like to be down there, get a feel for what's going on, and talk to the kids."

Paterno has always been in the thick of the action. In 2006 he spent one game in the press box after suffering a broken left leg at Wisconsin after he was run over during a play along the Penn State bench. And it was while showing some players how to kick the ball during a 2009 preseason practice session that the injury to his right leg occurred. By the third game Paterno needed a cane to walk and a golf cart to help him get around the practice field and to the press box.

Still, Paterno found some advantages coaching from the press box. "As far as making a significant contribution to the strategy side and on the tactical side, you're better off upstairs. You can see more," he said

But the head coach belongs on the sideline, and after a successful operation on his leg, that's where the 82-year-old Hall of Fame coach intends to be again in 2009—on the prowl in his black shoes and white socks.

Three short runs and it was first-and-goal at the 2. Fullback Dan Lawlor gained one, and Devlin was stopped for no gain on a sneak, but on third down Devlin plunged behind center A.Q. Shipley. The officials waited a few seconds as the players unpiled and then signaled a touchdown. Kevin Kelly's extra point made it 10–6 with 6:25 remaining.

The Buckeyes fumbled the kickoff inside the 10 and five plays later had to punt from their 28-yard line. The Lions used the clock and drove 48 yards for a 35-yard field goal with 1:07 left. Ohio State still had a chance. Three completed passes moved the ball from OSU's 20 to PSU's 43 with 45 seconds remaining. Then Pryor heaved a pass toward the right side of the goal line, but cornerback Lydell Sargeant stepped in front of Bryan Hartline for the interception in the end zone.

In Penn State's defensive terminology, Mark Rubin's safety position is known as "the Hero." Rubin was certainly the hero, not only that night in making the play of the game but also in the ultimate success of the Lions' Big Ten championship season.

Game Details

Penn State 13 • Ohio State 6

Penn State	0	3	0	10	**13**
Ohio State	0	3	3	0	**6**

Date: October 25, 2008

Team Records: Penn State 8–0, Ohio State 7–1

Scoring Plays:
PSU—Kelly 31-yard FG
OSU—Pettrey 41-yard FG
OSU—Pettrey 36-yard FG
PSU—Devlin one-yard run (Kelly PAT)
PSU—Kelly 35-yard FG

November 13, 2004

Standing Up for Paterno

Paul Posluszny Leads Goal-Line Stand

It may seem ludicrous that a goal-line stand against woeful Indiana is one of the greatest plays in Penn State's proud football history. In fact, at the time, in mid-November 2004, the bumbling Nittany Lions were not much better than Indiana, winning only one of their last 14 Big Ten games in two years, and that lone victory was over the pathetic Hoosiers.

But it was not the goal-line stand itself that was so significant but the context in which it occurred. It literally saved Joe Paterno's job.

Despite a legendary career that had produced two national championships and five undefeated teams since 1966, Paterno appeared to be losing his edge. Since the shocking late-season collapse of the No. 2 1999 team that seemed headed for another national championship game, the Lions had virtually stopped winning, with losing seasons in 2000, 2001, and 2003, and now again in 2004, with games still remaining against Indiana and Michigan State. Moreover, the way the team was playing and losing was embarrassing.

As the losses mounted, the media and fans increased their clamor for Paterno to retire for the good of the football program.

A defeat to Northwestern the Saturday before the Indiana game had marked the second year in a row that the Lions had lost their first six Big Ten games, and the two six-game losing streaks were the worst for Penn State since the school-record seven straight defeats in 1931.

A few days after the Northwestern loss, Penn State's president Graham Spanier and athletics director Tim Curley met secretly with Paterno at his home. That meeting and another similar one two weeks later that included two members of the university's board of trustees did not become public until more than a year later. When it did, Paterno revealed that he had been asked to step down.

"I had a couple of meetings with the people in the administration before the Indiana game that really—I wouldn't use the vernacular that we use in the locker room —but, I got P.O.'d," Paterno admitted to the *Pittsburgh Post-Gazette*. "I said, 'You guys just knock it off. If I can keep my staff together, we're going to surprise a lot of people.'"

No one realized how monumental the Indiana game would be, but it was another day filled with mistakes as two interceptions helped give IU a 13–7 halftime lead. Late in the third quarter, Penn State marched 81 yards to go ahead, only to see Indiana recapture the lead midway in the fourth period 16–14 on a 23-yard field goal. The Lions responded

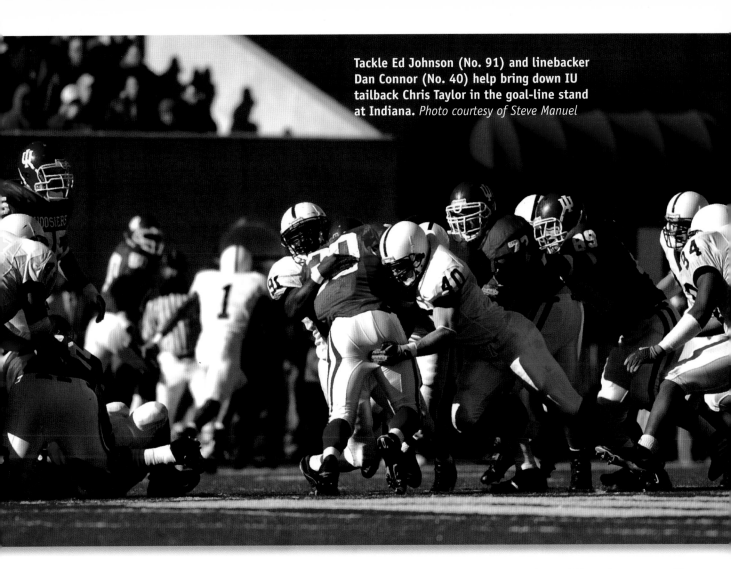

with an 80-yard drive that regained the lead 22–16 with 4:51 on the clock.

But Indiana's offense retaliated, going nearly 70 yards in five plays with a 29-yard pass completion on a third-and-9, putting the ball on State's 1-yard line with 2:13 remaining. Cornerback Anwar Phillips' tackle prevented the touchdown, making up somewhat for the pass interception he dropped moments earlier inside the Lions' 30 with an open field ahead of him. "When Anwar missed that," Paterno said, "I thought, *Here we go again.*"

Indiana lined up in a stacked I-formation with the three running backs behind the quarterback, and it would use that formation four straight times. On first down,

tailback Chris Taylor ran up the middle and was stopped by tackle Ed Johnson and linebackers Paul Posluszny, Derek Wake, and Dan Conner. On second down, it was Taylor again on the same play, and he was thrown for a one-yard loss with Posluszny at the point of the attack. The Lions called a timeout with 1:10 remaining. Quarterback Matt LoVecchio tried to cross up the Lions on third down with an option run to his right, but he was tackled by Wake and safety Calvin Lowry for no gain, and State used its final timeout with 59 seconds left.

On fourth down, the handoff once again went to Taylor charging up the middle. Johnson and tackle Scott Paxson hit Taylor low, and Posluszny plugged the hole, wrapping

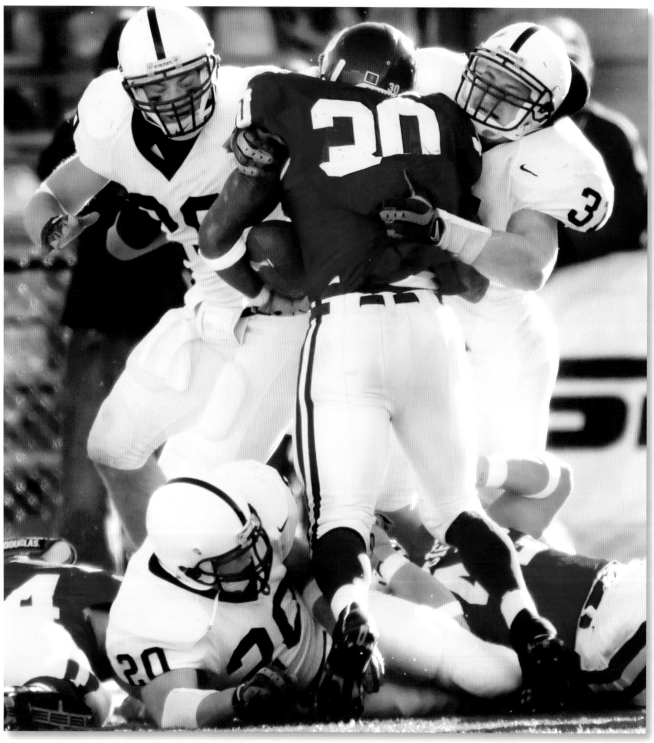

Linebacker Paul Posluszny (No. 31) leads the charge in the goal-line stand at Indiana in 2004. *Photo courtesy of* Blue White Illustrated *and Harvey Levine*

Linebacker U.

The history of Linebacker U. goes all the way back to 1906, when college football's patriarch, Walter Camp, selected center-linebacker William "Mother" Dunn as Penn State's initial first-team All-American. Since then, 14 Lions linebackers have been named first-team All-Americans, and seven others have been tabbed second- or third-team All-Americans.

But the Linebacker U. nickname didn't catch on until the success of dozens of Nittany Lions playing in the NFL in the 1960s and 1970s.

The best-known of all those linebackers is Jack Ham, an All-American in 1970 and an All-Pro with the Pittsburgh Steelers, who is the only Penn State player inducted into both the College and Pro Football Halls of Fame.

Sophomore Paul Posluszny and freshman Dan Connor were starters on the 2004 team. They were both chosen first-team All-Americans—Posluszny in 2005 and 2006 and Connor in 2006 and 2007. Both of them also won the Bednarik Award as college football's outstanding defensive player, and Posluszny won it twice. In his junior season Posluszny also won the Butkus Award as the nation's premier linebacker, following two-time All-American LaVar Arrington, who won the award in 1999.

Undoubtedly there will be more All-Americans coming out of Linebacker U. in the near future.

his arms around him as defensive backs Paul Cronin and Alan Zemaitis and their teammates smashed into the mass of bodies. The pile moved one yard but no more, and the jubilant Lions took over at the 6-inch line with 55 seconds showing on the clock.

Quarterback Zack Mills ran three plays into the line as Indiana used its last two timeouts. Then punter Jeremy Kapinos took the snap and scurried around the end zone before running across the end line for a safety as the clock ran out.

A year later, Paterno recalled his confrontation with his bosses: "I walked away that night…and there was one thing on my mind: We're going to get this team back to where it belongs."

> **T**hat's what you live for if you're a football player—goal-line stands like that.
>
> —DAN CONNOR

Game Details

Penn State 22 • Indiana 18

Penn State	7	0	7	8	22
Indiana	7	6	0	5	18

Date: November 13, 2004

Team Records: Penn State 2–7, Indiana 3–6

Scoring Plays:

IU—Roby 26-yard run (Robertson PAT)

PSU—Robinson 33-yard pass from Mills (Gould PAT)

IU—Killion 46-yard interception (kick failed)

PSU—Mills two-yard run (Gould PAT)

IU—Robertson 23-yard FG

PSU—Hunt two-yard run (Mills two-yard run)

IU—Safety (Kapinos ran out of end zone)

December 30, 1967

Paterno's Gamble Backfires in Gator Bowl

Lions Blow 17–0 Lead on Fourth-Down Play from Own 15-Yard Line

The play that made Joe Paterno a household name in the football world may have been one of the dumbest he ever called. Or maybe it was one of the smartest decisions of his career. It all depends on context and the effect the play had on Paterno's players.

Paterno was winding up his second season as Penn State's head coach, and after making some radical early season defensive changes that replaced veterans with inexperienced sophomores, the Nittany Lions had won their way into the Gator Bowl—then considered the most prestigious bowl after the New Year's Day games. However, there were still lingering doubts about Paterno's coaching ability. The skepticism was based partly on his mediocre first-year record of 5–5 but also on his continuing maneuvering of players from position to position and his constant fiddling

with the offensive and defensive formations and alignments. Everything still seemed too unsettled and uncomfortable.

Paterno was at it again during his preparations for the 1967 Gator Bowl. To negate the explosive passing offense of Florida State, Paterno closed practices and installed what he later called a shifting Y-formation on defense that resulted in multiple interchangeable alignments from a 5-3-3 and 6-2-3 to a 4-3-4 and 3-6-2. Players also switched positions on offense as well as defense, including at tight end, where All-American Ted Kwalick moved to wide receiver and often lined up on the same side as the new tight end and split end.

"The press wondered if Joe Paterno was pushing the panic button in his first bowl appearance," wrote Doug McDonald of the *Centre Daily Times*. "At halftime…Paterno looked like a genius."

Split end Jack Curry scores Penn State's first touchdown in the 1967 Gator Bowl. *Photo courtesy of Penn State Athletic Communications*

Paterno's imaginative defensive changes and the revitalized aggressiveness they had produced had confused Florida State, while the Seminoles also had problems coping with the Lions' versatile offense and its new wrinkles. Penn State was in complete control at halftime with a 17–0 lead, scoring touchdowns in the last five minutes of the second quarter on passes from Tom Sherman to Jack Curry for nine yards and Kwalick for 12 yards.

In the Penn State locker room, Paterno told his team "to play as if we're behind and have to make good on every down." His advice would come back to haunt him.

With some halftime adjustments, Florida State began moving the ball and about midway through the third quarter had a first-and-goal at the Lions' 3. But the Lions held, and after a fourth-down mix-up in the Seminoles' backfield, State took over at its 5-yard line. Moments later, it was the Lions with fourth-and–six inches near the 15 with 5:30 left in the quarter.

The Penn State punting team started onto the field but was called back when the Lions called timeout. On the sideline, many Penn State players wanted to go for it. Sherman led the offense back on the field, and up in the press box there was consternation, with the Penn State president, athletics director, and other school officials screaming, "What's he doing?" "He'd better not go for it!"

As 68,019 mostly Florida State fans and a national television audience watched on this warm, sunny afternoon, Sherman tried to sneak over his center. "I looked down, and the ball was more than a foot past the line," Sherman recalled after the game. "Someone caught the seat of my pants and pulled me back." And that's where the official spotted the ball when he turned and signaled a first down for Florida State.

Two plays later, Florida State had a touchdown, and after the Lions fumbled the ensuing kickoff at the 23, the Seminoles scored again to trail by just three points. Florida State had the momentum, but it couldn't crack Penn State's defense even as the Lions' offense sputtered. Then with 15 seconds remaining, the Seminoles had a fourth-and-4 at the State 9 after a 52-yard drive. They went for the tie and kicked a field goal.

Rival coaches Bill Peterson of Florida State (left) and Penn State's Joe Paterno joke before the 1967 Gator Bowl. *Photo courtesy of the Penn State Pattee-Paterno Library Sports Archives*

Bill Lenkaitis and Penn State Centers

The Nittany Lions have had many outstanding centers over the years, and no one was better than Bill Lenkaitis, the center at the crux of Joe Paterno's controversial Gator Bowl gamble.

Like quarterback Tom Sherman, Lenkaitis is still convinced that he and the guards alongside him, Dave Bradley and Bob Yowell, had made the first down on Sherman's quarterback sneak. Lenkaitis was a starting tackle in Paterno's first game in 1966, moved to center three games later, and stayed there the rest of his career.

Lenkaitis also had the best professional career of any Penn State center, even though he started out as a left guard when the San Diego Chargers drafted him second in 1968. In 1971 he was traded to the Patriots and was their starting center from mid-1973 almost to the day he retired after the 1981 season.

Although selected All-East in 1967, Lenkaitis never received the national recognition he should have.

Lenkaitis also went to dental school while playing pro ball and still has a dental practice in Foxboro, Massachusetts.

"I blew it," Paterno admitted after the game. "But if I ordered a punt on that play instead of a run I wouldn't have had the courage to be the football coach I want to be."

What Paterno had really done was show confidence in his players. And they knew it. Even though his gamble failed on the field, it was a success in the minds of his young players. Paterno's Nittany Lions would not lose or tie another game until three years later, and they would be the foundation for one of the most successful programs in college football.

"In the long run," Paterno said at the time, "that fourth-down call may be the best thing I ever did for Penn State football."

> **I** looked down, and the ball was more than a foot past the line. Someone caught the seat of my pants and pulled me back. Then the official came in, grabbed the ball, and spotted it where I was after being pulled. We made that first down.
>
> —TOM SHERMAN

Game Details

Penn State 17 • Florida State 17

Penn State	3	14	0	0	**17**
Florida State	0	0	14	3	**17**

Date: December 30, 1967
Team Records: Penn State 8–2,
Florida State 7–2–1

Scoring Plays:

PSU—Sherman 27-yard FG
PSU—Curry nine-yard pass from Sherman (Sherman PAT)
PSU—Kwalick 12-yard pass from Sherman (Sherman PAT)
FSU—Sellers 20-yard pass from Hammond (Guthrie PAT)
FSU—Hammond one-yard run (Guthrie PAT)
FSU—Guthrie 25-yard FG

This is an aerial view of the historic 1961 Gator Bowl on December 30, 1961, when Penn State's Dave Robinson became the first African American to play in the annual postseason game. *Photo courtesy of Penn State Athletic Communications*

December 30, 1961

Dave Robinson's "Play of the Century"

First African American in the Gator Bowl Makes an Unbelievable Play

The record crowd of 50,202 mostly partisan Georgia Tech fans in the Gator Bowl and the millions of people watching on national television could not believe what they had just seen. Penn State's junior defensive end Dave Robinson swept past a Georgia Tech blocker, grabbed the quarterback by the neck, and slammed him to the ground, jarring the football loose. And in a continuing split-second motion, Robinson picked up the ball and took a few steps before going down.

In the press box, Larry Merchant of the *Philadelphia Daily News* was awestruck. Merchant described what he had just witnessed as "possibly the play of the century."

Penn State was leading Georgia Tech 14–9 midway through the third quarter, when Robinson violently brought down quarterback Stan Gann and was tackled at the Tech 35-yard line. Without consulting with the coaches, quarterback Galen Hall again called the new play that had been inserted during pre-bowl practices. He faked a draw to tailback Roger Kochman, circled right, and threw a pass

to a wide-open Junior Powell at the 15-yard line. Powell's touchdown and Don Jonas' extra point broke the game open.

Yet the most meaningful achievement for Robinson that day in Jacksonville was not even mentioned in most stories of the game or in the pregame coverage by the media. This was a milestone day in college football, for on December 30, 1961, David Robinson of Moorestown, New Jersey, became the first African American to play in the Gator Bowl since the game was created in 1946. And it wasn't a pleasant experience, except for the game itself.

Because Jacksonville was a segregated city, the Penn State team stayed in St. Augustine, 25 miles south. En route from the north just after Christmas, the team had walked out of the Orlando airport restaurant, where Robinson was refused service. And even in St. Augustine, Robinson had to find a little restaurant in the small black section of the city because the drugstore where his white teammates hung out was unfriendly. On game day he was taunted with racial epithets and cursed by many of the fans. But he was surprised by the friendliness of the Georgia Tech players on the field. He learned years later that Tech coach Bobby Dodd had warned his team to be gentlemen.

"There were no incidents on the field whatsoever," Robinson remembered. "There was a lot of hard hitting but nothing out of the ordinary."

But he also remembers being upset because he did not start the game, only to learn later there had been a threat on his life by someone claiming to be an army sharpshooter.

Once on the field, he played the game of his life. Not only was he the defensive star of the game, but he was Penn State's leading pass receiver with four catches for 39 yards.

Tech had been a three-point favorite and jumped off to a 9–0 lead midway through the second quarter on a safety and a 68-yard touchdown run. But on its first possession after the Tech touchdown, State drove 78 yards to score on Hall's 13-yard pass to Al Gursky. With time running out in the half, the Lions blitzed downfield in a little over a minute and took the lead on Hall's 27-yard touchdown pass to Kochman and Jonas' kick. Then came Robinson's great play and Hall's quick touchdown pass.

Tech tightened the game early in the fourth quarter on an impromptu 23-yard touchdown run after a muffed pitchout. Then, with about six minutes remaining, Dodd tried a daring gamble on a fourth-and-6 at his team's 12-yard line, but the fake punt didn't work, and four plays later Jonas kicked a 23-yard field goal. On the first play following the kickoff, Jim Schwab intercepted Gann's pass at the Tech 20 and ran to the 11, and with a minute left and

All-American defensive end Dave Robinson integrated the Gator Bowl and made the "Play of the Century" in Penn State's 30–15 win over Georgia Tech. *Photo courtesy of Penn State Athletic Communications*

Dave Robinson: Linebacker U. Graduate

Dave Robinson was one of the early "graduates" of Linebacker U. in the years before Penn State acquired that nickname for producing so many All-American linebackers and NFL standouts. But he never did play linebacker as a Nittany Lion.

Basically a tight end on offense, Robinson was State's leading pass catcher as a junior. Robinson also played one of his finest defensive games in the 1962 17–7 Gator Bowl loss to Florida and was chosen as Penn State's Outstanding Player of the Game.

When Robinson joined the Green Bay Packers as their No. 1 draft choice in 1963, they moved him immediately to left linebacker and teamed him with veteran Ray Nitschke.

Nitschke is always named to the Packers All-Time team and is in the Pro Football Hall of Fame. However, Robinson is rarely named on the All-Time Packers teams and has been snubbed by Hall of Fame voters. In 1996 Dave Anderson, the now-retired and well-respected columnist of the *New York Times*, listed Robinson among what he called "The Hall of Fame's Forgotten 11."

In 1997 Robinson was inducted into the College Football Hall of Fame. That also was a long-overdue honor to the man who made history as the first African American to play in the Gator Bowl. Maybe someday the Pro Football Hall of Fame will remember him again, too.

four plays later, Buddy Torris bolted over for a one-yard touchdown.

Galen Hall was chosen the game's MVP, and Dodd told him at the awards banquet, "You are one of the greatest players a Tech team has had the privilege of playing against in my 17 years of coaching." That may have been true, but Dodd could have said the same words to the man who not only made "the play of the century" but made a strong statement for civil rights.

> **O**ne of their guards tried to take my legs out. He was coming so low I just went over him. I was still airborne when I struck the quarterback and he fumbled the ball. I would have scored, but in those days you couldn't advance a fumble. It was one of the turning plays of the game.
>
> —DAVE ROBINSON

Game Details

Penn State 30 • Georgia Tech 15

Penn State	0	14	6	10	**30**
Georgia Tech	2	7	0	6	**15**

Date: December 30, 1961

Team Records: Penn State 7–3, Georgia Tech 7–3

Scoring Plays:

GT—Safety (Hall threw pass from end zone)
GT—Auer 68-yard run (Lothridge PAT)
PSU—Gursky 13-yard pass from Hall (Jonas PAT)
PSU—Kochman 27-yard pass from Hall (Jonas PAT)
PSU—Powell 35-yard pass from Hall (Pass failed)
GT —Auer 23-yard run (pass failed)
PSU—Jonas 23-yard FG
PSU—Torris one-yard run (Jonas PAT)

November 5, 1955

Lenny Moore vs. Jimmy Brown

Hall of Fame Backs Duel at Beaver Field, but Defense and Kicking Plays Win Game

In Penn State's lengthy, prolonged climb through the decades to finally become one of the outstanding college football programs in the country, the Syracuse game at Beaver Field in 1955 seems like just one relatively small link in the long chain dating back to 1887. The final score had little impact on a mediocre 5–4 season, but what happened on the field that day is at the heart of the Nittany Lions' ultimate success.

The game is remembered as one of the true "classics" in Penn State's football history because of the exceptional all-around performances by two future Pro Football Hall of Fame backs, State's Lenny Moore and Syracuse's Jim Brown. It was one of the greatest duels ever in college football.

Brown was almost a one-man team, scoring all of Syracuse's 20 points. Yet, in the end, it was a gritty effort by a struggling junior quarterback who

would surpass Brown and Moore as the player of the game and a Lions team that twice overcame a 13-point deficit to win. And the big plays were made on defense, including Moore's touchdown-saving ankle tackle of Brown on the second-half kickoff.

Through most of the first half, it looked as if Syracuse would get its first win in the last 10 games at Beaver Field. State's quarterback was Milt Plum, who had been used mostly on defense that season but would, surprisingly, play nearly 60 minutes on this chilly, windy day. But when Plum fumbled at the State 29-yard line on the Lions' first possession, Brown ran for 27 of the yards needed to score, including the last two on fourth down, and then booted the extra point.

On the ensuing kickoff, the Lions reached the Syracuse 34 before giving up the ball on downs. With Brown doing the bulk of the running—and also catching a 15-yard pass—Syracuse scored again with Brown taking a six-yard pass for the touchdown.

Joe Paterno believes Lenny Moore is Penn State's greatest all-around football player, and his performance on offense, defense, and special teams against Syracuse in 1955 was his finest day ever. *Photo courtesy of Penn State Athletic Communications*

Then came the key play of the game. Penn State's sophomore third-string right end Jack Farls, playing only because of injuries, barreled through, and Brown's extra-point attempt caromed off Farls' chest. The block hardly roused the Penn State crowd.

As the second quarter was winding down, the Lions drove downfield behind the running of Moore before giving up the ball at the Syracuse 24. On third down from the 32 with less than 30 seconds left, Syracuse quarterback Ed Albright inexplicably tried a short sideline pass. State's Joe Sabol, another sophomore and third-team reserve, intercepted and raced down the sideline

Future Hall of Famer Jimmy Brown was a one-man scoring machine for Syracuse, but his blocked extra-point attempt was the difference in Penn State's 21–20 victory at Beaver Field in 1959. *Photo courtesy of AP Images*

to the Syracuse 10. With time expiring, Plum passed to backup right half Billy Kane in the left flat at the 2, and Kane ran in for the touchdown. Plum's extra point made it 13–7.

Brown was brought down by Moore at the Syracuse 47 on the second-half kickoff. The bruising junior then led the way on an eight-play drive, scoring from the 6 and kicking the extra point.

Something seemed to jell after Penn State took the short kickoff at its 41-yard line. In 11 plays with Moore, Kane, Sabol, and Plum making the plays, the Lions scored as Plum faked to Sabol at the 2 and gave the ball to Moore. Plum's kick made it 20–13 with 8:45 gone in the third quarter.

Minutes later, Brown intercepted Plum's pass at the Syracuse 41. On second down, Brown broke away for his longest run of the day, rambling 42 yards to the PSU 13 before being brought down from behind by

Game Details

Penn State 21 • Syracuse 20

Syracuse	7	6	7	0	**20**
Penn State	0	7	7	7	**21**

Date: November 5, 1955

Team Records: Penn State 3–3, Syracuse 3–2

Scoring Plays:

SYR—Brown two-yard run (Brown PAT)

SYR—Brown six-yard pass from Albright (Kick failed)

PSU—Kane 10-yard pass from Plum (Plum PAT)

SYR—Brown six-yard run (Brown PAT)

PSU—Moore two-yard run (Plum PAT)

PSU—Plum one-yard run (Plum PAT)

The Big Fight

Two years before the classic showdown between Lenny Moore and Jimmy Brown, Moore was at the center of the most bizarre ending of any Penn State–Syracuse game ever played. It was on the same Beaver Field on October 17, 1953.

Syracuse had taken a 14–0 lead late in the third quarter before the Lions snapped back to tie it up five minutes into the fourth quarter. As the game continued, the Lions stopped Syracuse at the State 21, but then both offenses bogged down and Syracuse had to punt from its own 34-yard line.

Moore went back to receive the punt. Syracuse seemed poised to go after Moore and underestimated the Lions' rush. Tackle Danny DeFalco blocked Albright's punt with his chest. Jim Garrity picked up the ball two yards away and ran 23 yards for the go-ahead touchdown.

However, Garrity missed his first extra-point kick of the season, and with the help of a short kickoff, a 15-yard penalty, and a quick pass completion, Syracuse had the ball at State's 40 with time for maybe a play or two. Backup quarterback Bruce Yancey threw a long pass toward the Lions' goal line. But Moore intercepted at about the 11-yard line and ran down the sideline in front of the Syracuse bench until he was pushed out of bounds at the 36 and almost disappeared into a mass of Syracuse players.

Jesse Arnelle, the Lions' big end who was one of Moore's closest friends, and several of his Lions teammates rushed into the Syracuse throng to help Moore, and suddenly the sideline erupted into a brawl. "I was pushed out of bounds and someone on the sideline jumped me with a cheap shot," Moore recalled years later.

There were 10 seconds left, and all the Lions had to do was run out the clock. But as Ridge Riley wrote in his weekly football newsletter sent to all Penn State alumni, "It was the longest 10 seconds ever experienced by the home crowd." That's because quarterback Don Bailey, who was known for his weird sense of humor, used an extraordinary long count and drew his own team offside on two consecutive plays.

Now, that truly was a unique way to end this football game.

Plum. Then Plum made amends for his interception by intercepting Albright in the end zone.

Then it was Moore's turn. After resting on the bench when the drive started, the senior left half carried the ball five times for 53 yards as Plum marched the Lions downfield in 11 plays and scored himself on a one-yard sneak. When Plum kicked the ball for the crucial extra point, he thought he had missed because the flight of the ball was low. But it barely cleared the crossbar, and State led for the first time 21–20 with four minutes remaining.

Syracuse fumbled away its last chance at its own 46, and Penn State had a first down at the Orange 1-yard line when the game ended. The happy crowd, many not realizing it had just witnessed a historic game, applauded both teams as they left the field. Lenny Moore and Jimmy Brown had turned it into a proverbial "classic."

But it was two unheralded third-string sophomores and a struggling junior quarterback who made it happen with three of the greatest plays in Penn State football history.

> It was Moore's greatest day. Did you see the movies? Well, they bear me out. Lenny was running hard, of course, but his blocking and tackling was of the best, too. Just sensational.
>
> —RIP ENGLE

December 29, 1989

Stealing the Holiday

Gary Brown Steals Ball from Ty Detmer in Wild Holiday Bowl Win

Penn State's wild 50–39 shootout victory over Brigham Young in the 1989 Holiday Bowl is far from being the most meaningful game in the Nittany Lions' football history, but it is arguably the most uniquely entertaining one.

The encounter in San Diego featured a record-setting aerial circus directed by a future Heisman Trophy winner; a leaping, acrobatic, off-a-face-mask reception labeled by ESPN's broadcaster as "the catch of the decade"; a 102-yard run for two points by an All-American linebacker that was the first ever under an obscure two-year-old NCAA rule allowing a team to score during an opponent's attempt for two points following a touchdown; and the brazen steal of the ball from the opposing quarterback's hands by a converted tailback now playing safety that resulted in a 53-yard touchdown with 48 seconds left and sealed the win.

Except for the Holiday Bowl passing records set by BYU's sophomore quarterback Ty Demeter, it was a Penn State player who dazzled the 61,113 sellout crowd in Jack Murphy Stadium and ESPN's national-television audience with those three breathtaking plays. And they all happened in the last five minutes of a slam-bang second half.

Penn State was playing in its first—and still only—Holiday Bowl and was happy to be there after blowing a chance at a New Year's Day game with tough losses to Alabama and Notre Dame and a disappointing tie with Maryland in the last half of the regular season. The Lions had rebounded from their first losing season in 50 years in 1988 and were eager to play BYU for the first time. The game was expected to pit State's run-oriented offense and its opportunistic defense against the passing wizardry of a BYU team that had won the Western Athletic Conference. No one expected a high-scoring, wide-open donnybrook.

The low-key, almost boring first half was no indication of the fireworks ahead after two field goals by both teams and a missed Penn State extra-point kick gave BYU a narrow 13–12 halftime lead. But when Lions freshman O.J. McDuffie ran back the second-half kickoff 46 yards to set up Ray Tarasi's career-long field goal of 51 yards that put the Lions ahead, the free-for-all was on.

For the rest of the third quarter the teams went up and down the field, trading touchdowns, including one by the Lions that was set up by a pass on a fake punt pulled off by a fake punter, flanker Terry Smith. Early in the fourth quarter, Penn State stretched a two-point lead into eight on

Gary Brown, seen here in a 1989 game at Texas, clinched Penn State's 50–39 victory over BYU in the Holiday Bowl by stealing the ball from quarterback Ty Detmer and running 53 yards for a touchdown. *Photo courtesy of Penn State Athletic Communications*

Gary Brown

Gary Brown epitomizes the football player who sacrifices himself for the benefit of the team.

Brown was a highly recruited running back who led Penn State in rushing as a sophomore when starter Blair Thomas sat out the season because of injuries. When Thomas returned for his final year in 1989, Penn State was loaded with backup running backs. Coach Joe Paterno asked Brown to fill a hole in the defensive backfield, and he willingly agreed.

Brown eventually started five games at the "Hero" position and climaxed his year in spectacular fashion in the closing moments of the Holiday Bowl. Paterno gave him his choice of positions for 1990, and Brown returned to tailback. Unfortunately, his fellow senior, Leroy Thompson, was entrenched as the starter, but Brown still finished second in rushing to Thompson and wound up playing in the 1991 Senior Bowl.

But Brown's sacrifice as a junior would be rewarded in the NFL, where he had a far better career than either Thompson or Thomas—who was the second overall player drafted in 1990. After being drafted in the eighth round by Houston in 1991, Brown spent eight years in the NFL and twice rushed for more than 1,000 yards, with Houston in 1993 and the New York Giants in 1998. He finished his career with 4,300 yards and 21 touchdowns—more than Thompson and Thomas had combined in their six NFL years.

Andre Collins was known for his hard tackling, but his 102-yard run for two points in the 1989 Holiday Bowl was one of the most unusual plays in Penn State history. *Photo courtesy of Penn State Athletic Communications*

a 73-yard touchdown drive, but a run for two points failed, and that would almost be fatal in the end.

Less than three minutes later, the Lions seemed to take a commanding 41–26 lead after an interception set up a spectacular 52-yard touchdown pass from Tony Sacca to Dave Daniels. Daniels, racing down the right sideline near the end zone, leaped over a defender and grabbed the ball, but it caromed off his hands as his body twisted, bounced off his face mask, off his hands again, and then onto his chest, where he clutched it firmly to his body and slid on his back through the end zone.

In the excitement, another miss for two extra points on a pass didn't seem important. But it became huge with 2:34 left in the game when BYU trailed by just 41–39 after two dynamic comeback touchdown drives led by Detmer. BYU was setting up to tie the score on its own two-point conversion attempt. Detmer threw to his tight end in the end zone, but Andre Collins jumped in front of him and without breaking stride was off and running, brushing aside the lone defender in his way—Detmer—and outracing everyone else across BYU's goal line for the two points permitted by the virtually unknown NCAA rule.

But BYU and Detmer weren't finished. The Cougars forced the Lions to punt for just the second time in the game, and in 30 seconds and four plays Detmer led BYU 68 yards to State's 38-yard line with less than a minute remaining. Penn State called for a blitz. Junior Gary Brown, the Lions' leading rusher in 1988 who had been switched from offense to safety in the preseason because of injuries (and would be back at tailback the following season), crashed from the blind side. Brown knocked down BYU's 6'5", 290-pound Outland Trophy winner Mohammed Elewonibi, stripped the ball from Detmer as he cocked his arm, and ran 53 yards for the game-clinching touchdown.

The frenetic game had lasted four hours and 17 minutes, and BYU's coach LaVell Edwards summed it all up perfectly for all those who were there or saw it on television: "That's the screwiest game I've ever been involved in."

It was a quiet, conservative game.
—JOE PATERNO, KIDDING REPORTERS

Game Details

Penn State 50 • Brigham Young 39

Penn State	3	9	17	21	**50**
Brigham Young	3	10	13	13	**39**

Date: December 29, 1989
Team Records: Penn State 7–3–1,
Brigham Young 10–2

Scoring Plays:
PSU—Tarasi 30-yard FG
BYU—Chaffetz 20-yard FG
PSU—Smith 24-yard pass from Sacca (kick failed)
BYU—Detmer one-yard run (Chaffetz PAT)
PSU—Tarasi 36-yard FG
BYU—Chaffetz 22-yard FG
PSU—Tarasi 51-yard FG
PSU—Thompson 16-yard run (Tarasi PAT)
BYU—Detmer one-yard run (kick blocked)
PSU—Thompson 14-yard run (Tarasi PAT)
BYU—Boyce 12-yard pass from Detmer (Chaffetz PAT)
PSU—B. Thomas seven-yard run (run failed)
PSU—Daniels 52-yard pass from Sacca (pass failed)
BYU—Whittingham 10-yard run (Chaffetz PAT)
BYU—Nyberg three-yard pass from Detmer (pass failed)
PSU—Collins 102-yard interception return off BYU
    (PAT failed)
PSU—Brown 53-yard return of stolen fumble (Tarasi PAT)

Special Teams Successes

October 20, 1956

The Game That Changed Penn State Forever

Milt Plum Leads Upset Over Defending National Champions

There is no more consequential game in the evolution of Penn State as one of the elite teams in college football than the shocking upset over Ohio State in Columbus in 1956. Sever "Tor" Toretti, the assistant coach who was the architect of the 7–6 victory, said years later that the game was the turning point that enabled the Nittany Lions to attract more talented and skilled players to win consistently on a national level. "Before that," Toretti said, "people would say, 'Penn State? Where the hell's that?'"

Not that Penn State didn't have some of those skilled athletes before, but certainly Ohio State had superior talent in 1956. With a veteran team that had won the national championship the previous season, the No. 5 Buckeyes had averaged 31 points and 333 yards in rolling over three opponents with a punishing ground game. Penn State had stomped two weak Eastern foes and lost to Army, 14–7, and by game day the Lions were a three-touchdown underdog.

The schools had not played since their first controversial game in 1912, when Penn State won 37–0. As in 1912, the OSU fans taunted the Penn State players before the game, and the 82,584 inside the Horseshoe was the largest crowd ever for a Penn State game up to that time.

Outweighed in player-to-player matchups, Engle decided to counter by playing two teams almost equally the entire 60 minutes. This was still the era where players had to play offense and defense. Quarterbacks also called their own plays, and Buckeyes quarterback Frank Ellwood would unknowingly help the Lions defense. Toretti discovered in scouting OSU that Ellwood tipped off his plays coming out of the huddle and in calling audibles. Maybe that's why the Buckeyes could mount only two serious scoring drives until the last minutes of the game.

Penn State's offense surprised Ohio State from the opening whistle and dominated the first half. Driving into the wind after OSU won the toss and kicked off, the Lions resembled the Buckeyes as they used mostly running plays to go 50 yards until a Milt Plum pass was intercepted at the Buckeyes' 10. The Buckeyes' fandom was stunned when

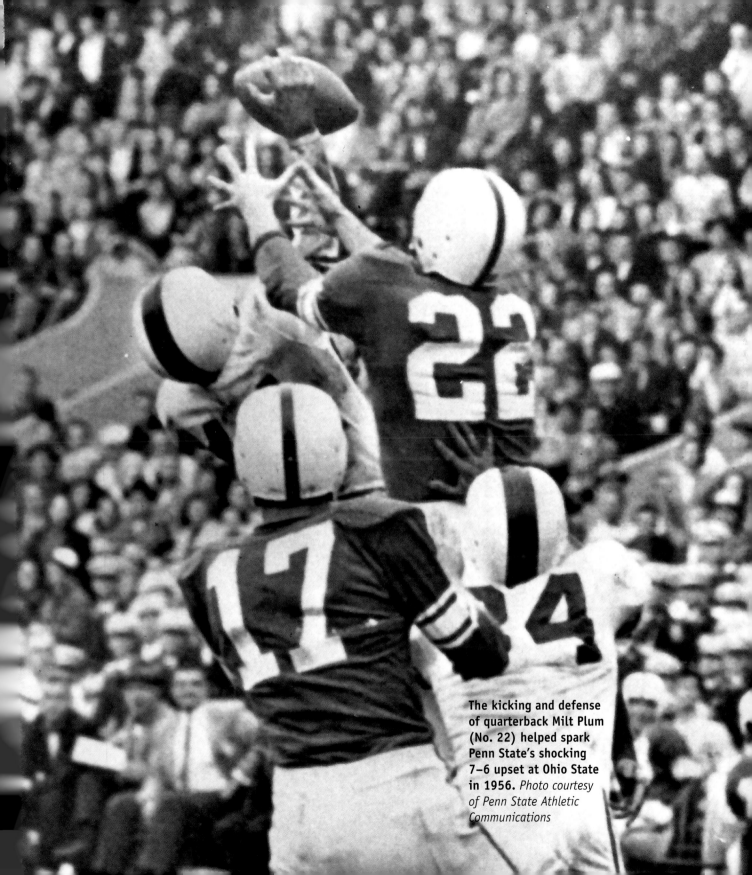

The kicking and defense of quarterback Milt Plum (No. 22) helped spark Penn State's shocking 7–6 upset at Ohio State in 1956. *Photo courtesy of Penn State Athletic Communications*

Linebacker and captain Sam Valentine, one of the defensive standouts against Ohio State in 1956, became coach Rip Engle's first-ever first-team All-American that season. *Photo courtesy of Penn State Athletic Communications*

the Lions immediately forced a punt and then went another 51 yards before another Plum pass was intercepted at the 2.

In the second quarter, a Penn State fumble at its own 45 led to a 25-yard field goal attempt by OSU's kicking specialist Frank Kremblas, but it was short and wide left. After the Lions reached midfield, Plum's booming 56-yard punt rolled dead at the Buckeyes' 1-yard line, and the Lions defense stymied OSU deep in its own territory for the rest of the half.

Penn State's offense did not let up, taking the second-half kickoff and reaching the OSU 13 before losing another fumble. Then the Buckeyes' offense finally woke up, pounding away upfield. At the Lions' 25, sophomore Don Clark broke into the clear but was tackled from behind by Lions sophomore Bruce Gilmore at the 5. On third-and-goal from the 3, Gilmore intercepted a pass into the end zone and ran it to the 21 as the third quarter came to an end.

The teams slugged it out in the fourth quarter until another thunderous punt of 71 yards by Plum rolled out at the Lions' 3. Penn State forced a punt, and the Lions took over at the OSU 45. On third-and-1, Plum juggled the ball on a handoff, so he kept it and ran 12 yards to the 24. Six running plays later, the Lions were at the 10, and Plum hit Billy Kane on a pass over the middle that was ruled down at the one-foot line. Gilmore banged over for the touchdown, and Plum calmly booted the extra point with 3:39 remaining.

Plum's kickoff went into the end zone, and after two running plays to their

The Buckeyes Quit in Columbus

The first time Penn State played Ohio State in 1912, the bizarre ending of the game strained relations so deeply the teams didn't meet again until 44 years later. And the man who helped arrange the second game, in 1956, was the Nittany Lions' captain in 1912 and a future Hall of Famer.

The pregame atmosphere was similar in both games, with Ohio State a heavy favorite to defeat the visitors from rural Pennsylvania. In 1912 Penn State shocked the Buckeyes from the start with a 16–0 first-quarter lead that kept increasing. It was a rough game with fists flying and blood flowing.

Penn State scored in the middle of the last quarter to push its lead to 37–0, and when a Buckeyes blocker was almost knocked out on the ensuing kickoff, Ohio State walked off the field, complaining of "unnecessary roughness." The officials told Penn State it would have to stay on the field for five minutes to claim the forfeit, and the police then had to protect the Lions from the angry partisan crowd.

State's captain, Pete Mauthe, went on to become president of a Youngstown steel company and the president of Penn State's board of trustees. Thanks to his mediation, the teams played again in 1956. One year later Mauthe became Penn State's first player inducted into the College Football Hall of Fame.

32, the Buckeyes crossed up the Lions with two quick halfback-option passes for 18 and 42 yards that suddenly put them on the State 3-yard line. Clark went off tackle for the touchdown, and coach Woody Hayes sent in Kremblas to tie the game with 1:58 left. But confusion over which player would come out led to a five-yard illegal-substitution penalty, and Kremblas' kick was wide again, as Ohio Stadium fell virtually silent. Penn State recovered the onside kick and ran out the clock.

Milt Plum's 71-yard punt and extra point were the difference in the game, and the sportswriters credited the Lions' ball control and its defense, led by linebackers Sam Valentine and Dan Radakovich, with being the backbone for the upset. "This will teach them a little more respect for Eastern football," said Rip Engle. He was quite prophetic.

Game Details

Penn State 7 • Ohio State 6

Penn State	0	0	0	7	7
Ohio State	0	0	0	6	6

Date: October 20, 1956
Team Records: Penn State 2–1, Ohio State 3–0

Scoring Plays:
PSU—Gilmore one-yard run (Plum PAT)
OSU—Clark three-yard run (kick failed)

I've never had a bigger victory.... This is the greatest bunch of kids I've ever coached. By maintaining control of the ball we took some zing out of Ohio State.

—RIP ENGLE

December 19, 1959

The Fake Field Goal That Beat the Bear

Roger Kochman Scores Only Touchdown in First Liberty Bowl

The 1959 State football team deserved a better reward for what it accomplished during the season, but it was all clouded by backroom Pennsylvania politics that forced the Nittany Lions to host the first Liberty Bowl game on a bitterly cold mid-December day in Philadelphia. Even so, the game produced one of the more intriguing plays in Penn State history.

Back then, bowl invitations were sent before teams had completed their schedules, and Penn State still had a game left with its bitterest rival, Pitt, when the bids went out from the eight postseason bowls. The players were disappointed when they were snubbed by the New Year's Day bowls, even though their only loss in eight games had been a 21–18 defeat to eventual national champion Syracuse two weeks earlier when both teams were undefeated and ranked in the top 10. The Gator Bowl—regarded as the best after the January 1 games— and the Bluebonnet Bowl had seemed interested but backed off after learning of the Liberty Bowl's manipulations. Distracted and demoralized, the Lions were upset 22–7 by a pumped- up 5–4 Pitt team and dropped out of the top 10.

Despite all the shenanigans leading up to the game, the focus of the matchup was on the two coaches, Penn State's Rip Engle and Alabama's Bear Bryant. This was Engle's best team since becoming the head coach in 1950 and his first to play in a bowl. Alabama's last bowl game had been in 1953 when Bryant was at Kentucky, where he had produced three bowl teams. Bryant had returned to Alabama as head coach in 1958, and although his 1959 team had lost only once with two ties, the Crimson Tide also had been forsaken by the New Year's

Sophomore Roger Kochman stumbles into the end zone on the last play of the first half for the only touchdown in Penn State's win over Alabama in the first Liberty Bowl. *Photo courtesy of the Penn State All-Sports Museum*

Day bowls, and he leaped at the chance to play Penn State in the Liberty Bowl.

By game day, the Penn State players realized this was their chance to redeem themselves. Even though the two teams had designed their game plans around the probability of bad weather, the 30-mile-an-hour winds made the wind chill far below freezing, and passing was almost impossible. The game turned into a classic defensive struggle, with both teams losing four fumbles and Alabama never getting past the Lions' 27-yard line.

Despite the miserable weather, Penn State missed three good scoring opportunities in the first half—fumbling at the Alabama 9-yard line, failing on a fourth-and-goal at the 1-yard line, and having a 22-yard field-goal attempt blocked. The Lions also lost their All-American quarterback, Richie Lucas, with a bruised hip early in the second quarter.

Then, with less than two minutes left in the first half, a short Alabama punt into the wind gave Penn State the ball at the Tide 22-yard line but with no timeouts remaining.

In preparing for his first bowl game, Engle had been advised by Georgia Tech coach Bobby Dodd to "put in some new plays." The Penn State coaching staff had seen a flaw in Alabama's rush on field-goal kicks, so four days before the game they devised a new screen pass off a fake field goal. Engle sent word to backup sophomore quarterback Galen Hall to "run a couple of plays" then use the fake-field-goal play. But after a drawn-out four-yard pass completion, there were just 18 seconds left when the Lions hurried to line up for a field-goal attempt.

Seeing that there was no tee for the place-kicker, the Alabama defenders yelled about a fake. What they didn't realize was this play was designed purposely with two fakes.

Charlie Janerette

The first Liberty Bowl was the first time ever that an Alabama football team had played against an opponent with a black player, Penn State senior tackle Charlie Janerette.

At the time, Janerette was the only African American on the Lions' roster. Janerette's forte was blocking, and in his senior year he was selected a second-team All-American by *Sporting News*. And before the Liberty Bowl was played, Janerette was drafted by the Los Angeles Rams.

Janerette was a native of the Philadelphia area, so his appearance in the Liberty Bowl was a homecoming and generated some publicity. Yet his race and the fact he would be the first African American to play against the segregated Alabama team was barely whispered. The most public notice was buried inside a few stories when the Tuscaloosa Citizens Council protested in a letter to Alabama's president, Frank Rose. "We strongly oppose our boys playing an integrated team," wrote council chairman James Laester. "The Tide belongs to all Alabama, and Alabamians favor continued segregation."

Janerette would play six years of pro football with four teams. Unfortunately he was shot by a Philadelphia policeman during a puzzling encounter in 1984, and his family was subsequently compensated after a negligent-death lawsuit.

Game Details

Penn State 7 • Alabama 0

Penn State	0	7	0	0	**7**
Alabama	0	0	0	0	**0**

Date: December 19, 1959
Team Records: Penn State 8–2, Alabama 7–1–2

Scoring Plays:
PSU—Kochman 18-yard pass from Hall (Stellatella PAT)

Hall, now the holder, had hardly practiced the play, and he took the snap with one second on the clock. He rolled to his right as the Lions' right end Norm Neff angled toward the sideline with the Alabama safety right with him. Three Alabama linemen broke through the State line and seemed ready to smash into the unprotected Hall. Suddenly, the quarterback spun around and threw the ball to sophomore halfback Roger Kochman, who had brush-blocked a Tide lineman, and then darted toward the left sideline.

Kochman was wide open at the 6-yard line with three blockers in front of him. He caught the pass and stumbled into the end zone as a fourth blocker, the erstwhile receiver Neff, wiped out the last two Alabama defenders. Sam Stellatella booted the extra point, and that was it. The second half was anticlimactic, with neither team able to move the ball until near the end when State marched to the Tide 5-yard line as time expired.

Alas, the 7–0 win didn't help Penn State in the final polls, which had been released December 7, but the fake field goal that beat the Bear will be remembered for decades.

> **It** was just a well-executed play. They fooled us on it completely.
>
> —ALABAMA COACH PAUL "BEAR" BRYANT

Tackle Charlie Janerette (sixth from the left), seen here with Penn State's starting lineup at the 1959 Liberty Bowl, was the first African American to play against Alabama. *Photo courtesy of Penn State Athletic Communications*

November 11, 1978

No. 1 at Last

Matt Bahr Field Goals and Matt Suhey's Punt Return Boost Lions to No. 1 for First Time

Because the 1978 team had the misfortune of losing the national championship in dramatic fashion in a disappointing showdown game with Alabama at the Sugar Bowl, its crucial plays during that otherwise outstanding season are almost forgotten.

One gets the sense that the crestfallen Penn State nation not only wants to erase the memory of Alabama's goal-line stand on New Year's night but also everything else about that season when the Nittany Lions became the No. 1 team in the country for the first time.

The Lions had been a consensus No. 3 in the preseason polls, and they breezed through nine opponents with only one stumble, needing to overcome a nine-point deficit in the third quarter at Beaver Stadium to defeat SMU 26–21 in game four. But that was all but forgotten the week before the NC State game, when the Lions overwhelmed No. 5 Maryland 27–3 in a so-called "Battle of the Unbeatens" that moved State up to No. 2 behind Oklahoma and landed State's quarterback and Heisman Trophy candidate Chuck Fusina on the cover of *Sports Illustrated*.

Perhaps it was the euphoria left over from Maryland that caused the listlessness and sloppiness in the first half against 17-point underdog NC State. The fans were also somewhat apathetic because the smallest crowd of the year turned out—just a week after a new Beaver Stadium attendance record had been set, thanks to 16,000 new seats added before the start of the season.

The 77,043 partisans watched as the Lions offense that had been averaging nearly 33 points and about 400 total yards a game, bumbled its way through the first 30 minutes, squandering four scoring opportunities and getting just a 33-yard Bahr field goal in the second quarter. Late in the half, a NC State interception set up a short 28-yard touchdown drive that put the Wolfpack ahead with eight seconds remaining, and for the first time since SMU, Penn State was behind at the half.

The Lions offense perked up after the intermission, but NC State forced them to settle for three more Bahr field goals in the third quarter that gave Penn State a 12–7 lead. Less than two minutes into the fourth period, the Wolfpack narrowed the margin with their own

42-yard field goal, and as the clock wound down, the crowd became noticeably edgy.

With about six minutes left, the press box came alive with the news that Nebraska had upset No. 1 Oklahoma. But the battle down on the Beaver Stadium turf was too intense, and Penn State's officials decided to withhold the result from the public. The Lions were within minutes of finally reaching college football's summit after 91 years, and just the small cadre of fans listening on their transistor radios inside the stadium knew it.

Two minutes later the Penn State defense forced NC State to punt from near its goal line. Suhey and Mike Guman dropped back, and Guman hollered at Suhey, who was on his right, to make a fair catch. Suhey never heard him. Suhey already had run back four punts and had almost broken away for touchdowns on two of them.

Suhey said later that Guman "was probably right because the guy was right on top of me when I made the catch." Suhey took the ball at the NC State 43-yard line, evaded the would-be tackler, thrust his right arm down

A fourth-quarter punt return by Matt Suhey, shown here diving for a touchdown, sealed Penn State's 1978 win over NC State that made Penn State No.1 in the polls for the first time. *Photo courtesy of Penn State Athletic Communications*

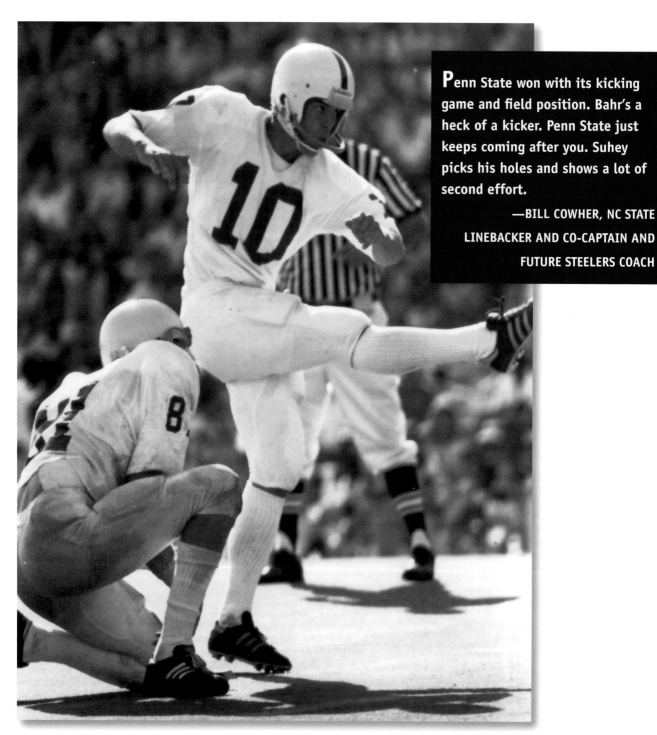

Penn State won with its kicking game and field position. Bahr's a heck of a kicker. Penn State just keeps coming after you. Suhey picks his holes and shows a lot of second effort.

—BILL COWHER, NC STATE LINEBACKER AND CO-CAPTAIN AND FUTURE STEELERS COACH

Matt Bahr's field goals were a deciding factor in Penn State's victory over North Carolina State on November 11, 1978. *Photo courtesy of the Penn State Pattee-Paterno Library Sports Archives*

The Brothers Suhey

More than a dozen brothers have played football for Joe Paterno, and the story of each family is different. Take the Suhey brothers, who played on Paterno's teams in the 1970s.

Larry, Paul, and Matt Suhey have a unique Penn State legacy. Their grandfather, Bob Higgins, was a two-time Penn State first-team All-American and longtime coach, and their father, Steve, was a first-team All-American who played for Higgins on the Nittany Lions' undefeated Cotton Bowl team of 1947. Both Higgins and Steve Suhey are in the College Football Hall of Fame. And the Suhey brothers' tie to Paterno goes back to their births, because Paterno roomed at the Suhey home when he first went to Penn State as an assistant coach in 1950.

The Suhey brothers played one year together at Penn State. That was in 1976, when Larry was a senior and the designated starting fullback, until injuries sidelined him for several games. Matt, a freshman in 1976, played at tailback and fullback during his career, and Paul was a linebacker and co-captain of the 1978 team.

Matt is the only brother who played professional football. He had a distinguished 10-year NFL career as the starting fullback for the Chicago Bears and scored the first touchdown in the Bears' Super Bowl win over New England in 1985.

And the Suhey legacy continues. Matt's son, Joey, is a redshirt sophomore running back on Paterno's 2009 team.

---

on the grass to regain his balance, and ran toward the left sideline as his blockers, including his brother Paul, a co-captain and linebacker, cleared an open path. There was 3:38 remaining in the game when Suhey scored and Bahr kicked the extra point.

As the crowd was settling down, the public-address announcer told them that Oklahoma had lost, and fans were back on their feet yelling and screaming, with their arms and index fingers raised high above their heads.

The Penn State defense made sure NC State was finished. When the game was over, the defense could boast about limiting the Wolfpack's standout runner Ted Brown to 71 yards after he had rushed for a record 251 yards against the Lions in 1977. Bahr could boast about the four field goals that gave him 21 for the season, tying an NCAA record. Suhey could boast about the first touchdown he ever scored on a punt return—including high school—which clinched the game and kept the Lions in contention for the national championship.

And three days later, when the Associated Press and United Press rankings came out, Penn State fans all over could finally—and officially—boast: "We're No. 1!"

Game Details

Penn State 19 • North Carolina State 10

NC State	0	7	0	3	**10**
Penn State	0	3	9	7	**19**

Date: November 11, 1978
Team Records: Penn State 9–0,
North Carolina State 6–2

Scoring Plays:
PSU—Bahr 33-yard FG
NCS—Brown 20-yard run (Ritter PAT)
PSU—Bahr 32-yard FG
PSU—Bahr 37-yard FG
PSU—Bahr 30-yard FG
NCS—Ritter 42-yard FG
PSU—M. Suhey 43-yard punt return (Bahr PAT)

November 18, 1995

Faking Out Michigan in the Snow

Fake Field Goal in Fourth Quarter Beats Michigan in "Snow Bowl"

The surprise 18-inch snowfall that required a small battalion of paid volunteers and prison inmates to clear out Beaver Stadium so that the game could be played is one reason the 1995 clash with Michigan is one of the most memorable in Penn State history. Equally unforgettable is the way the game was decided—on a fan-pleasing trick play late in the fourth quarter that the Wolverines knew was coming and had prepared for but still couldn't stop. It would be the last time Penn State would defeat Michigan at home for the next 13 years—a depressing stretch that included four straight losses at Beaver Stadium and another five defeats in a row in Ann Arbor.

Until that frigid afternoon in mid-November, the 1995 season had been a major disappointment. After going undefeated, winning the Big Ten championship and the Rose Bowl, and finishing No. 2 in the polls in 1994, the veteran Lions, with 44 lettermen returning, had been ranked No. 4 in the preseason. But close back-to-back early season losses at home to Wisconsin and Ohio State and a solid whipping by upstart Northwestern in their previous game two weeks earlier at Evanston made the game against No. 14 Michigan pivotal to salvaging the year. A probable New Year's Day game in the Outback Bowl as the Big Ten's third-place team was anticipated for the winner.

With an open date and an extra week to prepare, the 19th-ranked Lions spent more time practicing a fake field goal based on a specific defensive formation Michigan

Volunteers clear the snow from the seats and field
of Beaver Stadium for the 1995 Michigan game.
Photo courtesy of Dave Bentz

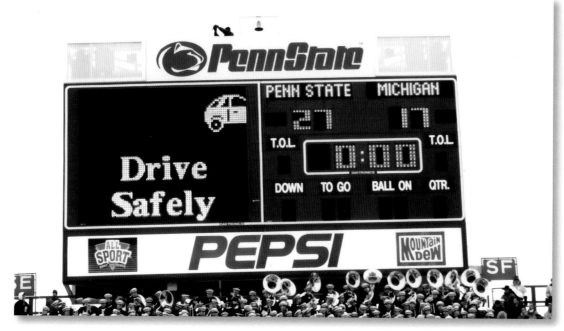

The scoreboard shows the final score as time runs out in Penn State's 27–17 victory over Michigan in the Snow Bowl. *Photo courtesy of Steve Manuel and Penn State Athletic Communications*

sometimes used. "We practiced the play all week," holder Joe Nastasi said later. Michigan's first-year coach Lloyd Carr also had a hunch Penn State might try a fake kick at some point because of weather conditions, and he had the Wolverines practice against it.

There might not have been any need for the fake if Penn State had not fumbled away two opportunities to break the game open. Leading 10–0 midway through the second quarter after a 49-yard field goal and 83-yard touchdown drive, the Lions lost a fumble at the Wolverines' 9 that Michigan turned into a 91-yard touchdown drive of its own. Then with the score 20–10 early in the fourth quarter, sophomore tailback Curtis Enis fumbled into the end zone on a handoff at the 1-yard line.

However, on their next possession the Lions went 57 yards for a score on Wally Richardson's 12-yard pass to All-American Bobby Engram, only to see Michigan narrow the margin to three points again with a quick 73-yard, six-play drive with 7:12 remaining on the clock.

When tailback Stephen Pitts surprised the Wolverines with a juking 58-yard run that set up a first-and-goal at the Michigan 8 with 4:08 left, another Lions touchdown looked probable. But three plays later, the ball was on the

2, and Nastasi, a virtually unknown redshirt sophomore, jogged into the south end of the stadium with field-goal kicker Brett Conway, who had booted the longest field goal of his career, 51 yards, in the second quarter.

Before Conway's two earlier field goals, Nastasi noticed Michigan lining up in its vulnerable formation, but he didn't call for the fake because he was unsure it would work and was not confident that Paterno would want it in those circumstances. This time Paterno and offensive coordinator Fran Ganter told him on the sideline to make the call if the formation was there.

Paterno and Ganter figured a successful field goal would give the Lions only a six-point lead, and they were wary of the resurging Michigan offense. "Timing is everything," Paterno said later. "It's not what you call but when you call it."

Michigan smelled a fake. Carr was hollering from the sideline, and some his defenders picked up the mantra, yelling, "Watch the fake. Watch the fake." "We were kind of looking for it," Michigan nose tackle Jason Horn said later.

Nastasi kneeled down about six yards behind long snapper Keith Conlin, scanned the formation, and called

Joe Nastasi: A Footnote in Recruiting History

Joe Nastasi's name may not be familiar to college football fans, but he's a historical figure in the competitive and mercurial world of high school recruiting.

Nastasi is the first known high school player to accept a college football scholarship before his senior season. The now-popular practice of getting early commitments has developed into a big business for the media, who report on it ad nauseam year-round.

Phil Grosz is publisher of one such online and print outlet, *Blue-White Illustrated*. "I've been covering recruiting for nearly 30 years, and Nastasi was the first person who publicly made a statement that he wanted to make a commitment in the spring of his junior year in school," said Grosz. "All the other guys who follow recruiting agree that Nastasi started the whole thing."

That happened in the spring of 1993. Nastasi was a wide receiver from nearby Bedford. He had recruiting letters from several schools in the East, but he decided on Penn State. "Joe [Paterno] and I talked, and I made the commitment," Nastasi said. "I didn't think it was any big deal."

It hadn't been done before because of an unwritten agreement between high school and college coaches. But Nastasi's coach was happy. His name is Joe Nastasi Sr.

---

the audible. As 80,000 shivering fans and a national-television audience watched, Nastasi took the snap and took off toward his right with All-American guard Jeff Hartings and subtackle Pete Marczyk clearing the way.

"The blocking was perfect," Nastasi said in the locker room. "I looked up and saw a big hole."

Michigan still had a shot with 2:40 remaining, but the Lions' defense ended it all at the PSU 45 after forcing four incomplete passes.

Penn State went on to beat Michigan State in a last-minute, come-from-behind thriller and then trounced Auburn 43–14 in the heavy rain at the Outback Bowl to finish 13th or 14th in the three major polls. Joe Nastasi and the fake field goal that beat Michigan was now an unforgettable part of the Nittany Lions lore.

> **I** told [wide receiver] Freddy Scott Friday night I was going to take one to the house. He said I'd probably get caught from behind.
>
> —JOE NASTASI

Game Details

Penn State 27 • Michigan 17

Michigan	0	7	3	7	**17**
Penn State	0	13	7	7	**27**

Date: November 18, 1995
Team Records: Penn State 6–3, Michigan 8–2

Scoring Plays:
PSU—Conway 49-yard FG
PSU—Archie 13-yard pass from Richardson (Conway PAT)
UM—Toomer 18-yard pass from Griese (Hamilton PAT)
PSU—Conway 51-yard FG
UM—Hamilton 29-yard FG
PSU—Engram 12-yard pass from Richardson (Conway PAT)
UM—Biakabutuka 18-yard run (Hamilton PAT)
PSU—Nastasi two-yard run on fake FG (Conway PAT)

November 17, 1990

The Freshman Who Booted Notre Dame from No. 1

Craig Fayak's 34-Yard Field Goal on Last Play Upsets Irish

Pulling off an upset over the No. 1 team in the nation is always exhilarating, but it's even more so when it comes down to a field goal by a true freshman kicker against one of college football's most glamorous teams in their own stadium on the last play of the game.

It's one of those stereotypical Hollywood endings that young men dream about from the time they begin tossing a football around in their backyards. But for Craig Fayak, the dream turned into reality.

As Fayak stood under the glaring artificial lights of Notre Dame Stadium on that cold, early evening in mid-November 1990, the 18-year-old kicker thought back to his home in Belle Vernon, outside Pittsburgh. He looked at the scoreboard. There were eight seconds left on the clock, and the game was tied 21–21. Notre Dame had just called a timeout, and the noisy partisan crowd was trying

to disrupt his concentration as an ESPN television audience watched. Fayak leaned forward to show his holder, Bill Spoor, where to place the ball on the 34-yard line, and he calmly said to him, "Hey, it's just like kicking in my backyard. I have a goal post there, and I've made this kick a million times."

Spoor couldn't believe it. But Fayak wasn't kidding. He also remembered the last time he had kicked the winning field goal on the last play of the game. He was nine years old, and it was a midget football game.

But this was Notre Dame, perhaps the most famous name in college football. And earlier, in the third quarter, Fayak had missed a 39-yard field goal. "Sure, I was very nervous at first when we intercepted the ball and I realized I'd have to go in and kick," Fayak recalled years later, "but once I stepped on the field that all went away. I was very confident."

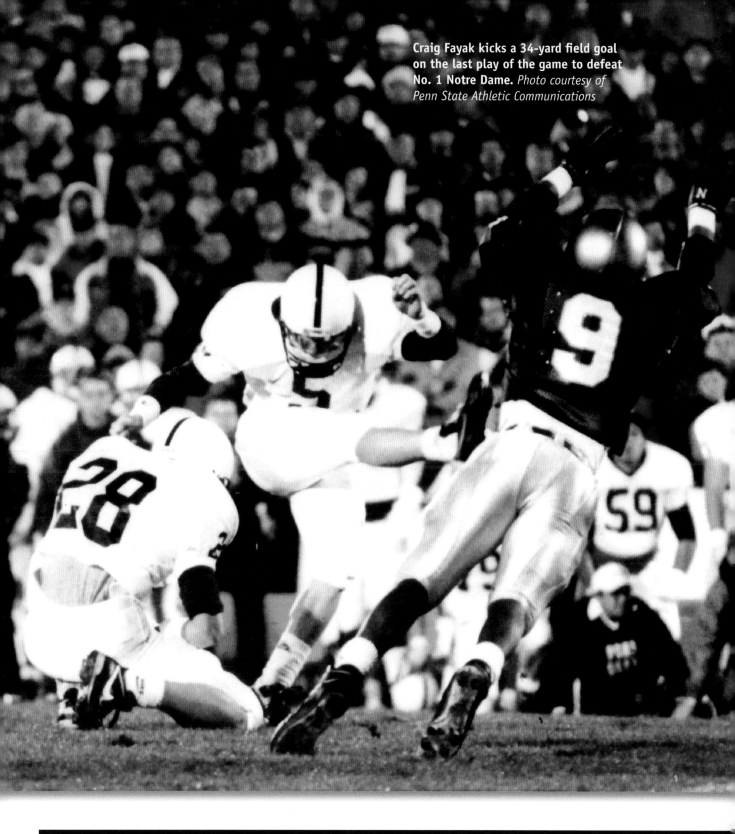

Craig Fayak kicks a 34-yard field goal on the last play of the game to defeat No. 1 Notre Dame. *Photo courtesy of Penn State Athletic Communications*

Fayak's truly golden opportunity came because his teammates had overcome a horrendous start in the first half. Notre Dame bolted to a 14–0 lead in the first eight and a half minutes on sustained drives of 63 and 59 yards and then used a relentless 92-yard, 16-play march in the first quarter to take a 21–7 score into the intermission. Only a 62-yard Penn State drive in the first quarter prevented the margin from being bigger.

As the second half started, the seven-game winning streak that had moved Penn State to No. 18 in the polls after two opening-season losses was in jeopardy. But there was one bad omen for the Irish. Their prolific playmaker, flanker Raghib "Rocket" Ismail, would not play the second half because of a deep thigh bruise. He had burned the Lions in the first half for 109 yards on 10 possessions as a receiver, runner, and kick returner, and his absence would be a big break for State.

Without Ismail, Notre Dame's offense sputtered, but State's reenergized defense came out of the locker room and took charge immediately. Near the end of the third quarter, linebacker Mark D'Onofrio intercepted a Rick Mirer pass and returned it 38 yards to the Notre Dame 11. On third down, quarterback Tony Sacca hit Ricky Sayles tip-toeing near the end line of the end zone for a touchdown. Midway through the fourth quarter, the Lions tied the game at 21–21 on Fayak's third PAT after Sacca's 14-yard touchdown pass to Al Golden capped a 58-yard drive.

Notre Dame had not crossed midfield in the second half as the Lions pressed their attack, but with 2:35 left in the game, the Irish had State facing a fourth-and-2 from the Notre Dame 37. "If we don't make it and they get a couple of first downs, they have one of the best kickers in the country, and I wasn't going to give them the game," Paterno recalled later.

Punter Doug Helkowski pinned the Irish at the 7-yard line, but on the first play they ran for a first down at the 17. They would get no further. On third down Mirer overthrew his receiver over the middle. Safety Darren Perry intercepted at the 39 and ran it back 20 yards. There were just 59 seconds left. Two running plays moved the ball to the middle of the field at the 34, and Fayak trotted out from the sideline.

"I knew it was good as soon as I hit it," Fayak said. "I saw the trajectory, and I knew it was right down the gut."

Fayak's melodramatic kick helped Penn State finish the 1990 season with its best record since winning the national championship in 1986. Fayak will always be known in Penn State history as the kicker who booted Notre Dame from No. 1.

> **B**efore we left home I told my roommate [Kyle Brady] that I had a feeling it was going to come down to me. It didn't bother me when they called timeout. It gave me a chance to think about it, to calm myself down.
>
> —CRAIG FAYAK

Game Details

Penn State 24 • Notre Dame 21

Penn State	7	0	7	10	**24**
Notre Dame	14	7	0	0	**21**

Date: November 17, 1990

Team Records: Penn State 7–2, Notre Dame 8–1

Scoring Plays:
ND—Watters 22-yard run (Hentrich PAT)
ND—Brooks 12-yard run (Hentrich PAT)
PSU—Smith 32-yard pass from Sacca (Fayak PAT)
ND—Mirer one-yard run (Hentrich PAT)
PSU—Sayles 11-yard pass from Sacca (Fayak PAT)
PSU—Golden 14-yard pass from Sacca (Fayak PAT)
PSU—Fayak 34-yard FG

Craig Fayak and What Might Have Been

After kicking his historic winning field goal against Notre Dame and setting Penn State scoring records in his freshman and sophomore seasons, Craig Fayak seemed destined to become the school's greatest place-kicker with a potentially outstanding NFL career ahead of him.

But a quirky back injury midway through his junior year changed everything. Before the 1992 season, Fayak began to lift weights to get stronger. As the season unfolded, he was doing some of his best kicking and after five games had a string of 13 straight field goals. But he began having serious back spasms.

In a showdown of unbeaten teams at Beaver Stadium in early October between No. 5 Penn State and No. 2 Miami, Fayak missed two field goals and had another blocked as Miami won 17–14. The back problem forced him to the sideline the rest of the year, and he struggled through pain as a senior.

What he didn't realize until it was too late was that his style and technique of his kicking collided with his weight-lifting technique, and his vertebrae started to crack. "It was a painful injury, and I was really never the same."

Fayak made his last Penn State kick in the 1994 Citrus Bowl victory over Tennessee, booting a 19-yard field goal and four extra points in a 31–13 victory. He still held the team's career scoring record until his 282 points were surpassed by Kevin Kelly in 2007.

Craig Fayak celebrates after his successful 34-yard field goal against Notre Dame on November 17, 1990. *Photo courtesy of Penn State Athletic Communications*

November 7, 1959

Missing the Point and the Prize

100-Yard Kickoff Return and Blocked Kick Almost Pull Out Victory

A missed extra point changed everything, or Penn State might have been the national champion in 1959 instead of Syracuse when the two teams played in what was the most significant game ever at New Beaver Field. It was hyped as the "Battle of Unbeatens" with both teams in the top 10—the Lions at No. 7 and the Orange at No. 3—and a New Year's Day bowl game was the prize.

Beaver Field, located in the center of campus, would be replaced after the season by a new stadium nearly a mile and a half away, and the largest crowd in the history of the 50-year-old facility—34,000—witnessed a classic. In the end, it came down to a dramatic fourth-quarter comeback by Penn State that fell short.

It didn't seem like much when Sam Stellatella missed his second extra point of the

season 11 minutes into the game. A Syracuse fumble at its own 45-yard line had led to Penn State's touchdown on a 17-yard run by sophomore reserve halfback Roger Kochman.

But Syracuse, favored by six points, then took charge. With sustained drives of 45, 56, and 41 yards, the Orangemen built up a 20–6 lead but also missed an extra-point kick after the third touchdown with 11:20 left in the fourth quarter. What happened in the next few seconds stunned everyone.

Kochman took the Syracuse kickoff on the goal line and sped up the middle behind his blockers, cut to the right when sprung by an Earl Kohlhaas block, broke two tackles, and outran sophomore Ernie Davis—the future Heisman Trophy winner—and another Orange defender. Bedlam broke out all over Beaver Field, but it quieted down when quarterback Richie Lucas' hurried pass for two points fell short.

Andy Stynchula's blocked punt in the fourth quarter leads to a Penn State touchdown in 1959's classic "Battle of the Unbeatens" against Syracuse at Beaver Field. *Photo courtesy of Penn State Athletic Communications*

As the tension continued with the clock ticking down in the 30-degree weather, the teams traded possessions, and with less than five minutes to play, Syracuse was forced to punt from its own 9-yard line. The partisan crowd was about to see another stunner. Left tackle Andy Stynchula—a future starter for the Washington Redskins—broke across the line, smashed into three Orange blockers, leaped high with his knee in one blocker's back, and batted the ball with his right forearm.

Players scrambled to get the ball. Just as Syracuse's All-American Fred Mautino was about to pick it up, he was blasted by fullback Sam Sobczak, and Lions end Bob Mitinger fell on the ball at the 1-yard line. The crowd was still roaring when Sobczak went up the middle for the touchdown. Now, two points would tie the game with 4:15 remaining. Lucas called the same play that had produced State's first touchdown, faking a roll out to the left but giving the ball to Kochman. This time a mass of tacklers stopped Kochman short of the goal.

There was too much time left for an onside kick, but when Davis took the ensuing kickoff and absentmindedly stepped out of bounds at the Syracuse 7, it looked as if things were continuing to go Penn State's way. But the Syracuse offense didn't break, picking up two first downs as it ran out the clock for the 20–18 victory. As the two teams left the field, the emotionally drained but

End Bob Mitinger was a scourge on defense for the 1959 Nittany Lions and became a first-team All-American. *Photo courtesy of Penn State Athletic Communications*

New Beaver Field

New Beaver Field was Penn State's third playing site for football, and a crowd of 500 was there on October 2, 1909, when the Nittany Lions christened the facility by beating Grove City 31–0 for their 100th all-time victory.

Like its predecessor—Old Beaver Field—and successor—Beaver Stadium—the complex was named after one of the university's most important benefactors, James A. Beaver. A lawyer by trade, Beaver was a Pennsylvania governor and Civil War general who also served on the Penn State Board of Trustees for more than 25 years and was once the interim president of the college.

From 1931 through 1939 Beaver Field's wooden grandstands were replaced with steel stands that gradually refigured seating capacity at 13,800. Then in 1949 permanent seats were built at the north end zone, turning the facility into a horseshoe with temporary bleachers in the south end. That made the final seating capacity 28,000 with standing room capping out at 34,000.

Seven days after Penn State's historic game with Syracuse, the Nittany Lions played their last game in New Beaver Field and beat Holy Cross 46–0, giving them a final record of 183–34–11 in the grand old stadium. Two days later, contractors began dismantling the steel structure and moving it in 700 pieces a mile and a half east to a one-time cow pasture where it would be rebuilt, expanded, and renamed Beaver Stadium when it opened the next season.

appreciative Beaver Field crowd stood and applauded for several minutes.

"That Penn State team was the greatest team I've ever come up against," said a gracious winning coach, Ben Schwartzwalder, in the locker room.

Syracuse jumped to No. 1 after losses that weekend by LSU and Northwestern, and at the end of the regular season would be declared national champions in the AP and UPI polls. A demoralized Penn State team would be upset by Pitt in its final regular-season game of the year and finish No. 11 and No. 10 in the final rankings.

Missed extra points made the difference.

> **I** just ran where there wasn't anyone...I saw an opening to the right and headed for it...I thought someone would catch me...I just wanted to get the end zone as fast as I could.
>
> —ROGER KOCHMAN

Game Details

Syracuse 20 • Penn State 18

Penn State	6	0	0	12	**18**
Syracuse	0	7	7	6	**20**

Date: November 7, 1959

Team Records: Penn State 7–0, Syracuse 6–0

Scoring Plays:

PSU—Kochman 17-yard run (Stellatella kick failed)

SYR—Schwedes six-yard pitchout from Sarette (Yates PAT)

SYR—Baker five-yard pass from Sarette (Yates PAT)

SYR—Davis two-yard run (kick failed)

PSU—Kochman 100-yard kickoff return (pass failed)

PSU—Sobczak one-yard run (run failed)

October 27, 2001

Paterno Snags His Bear

Last-Minute Blocked Field Goal Makes Paterno Winningest Coach in History

It seemed inevitable at the end of the 1999 season that Joe Paterno would pass Alabama's Paul "Bear" Bryant as the winningest coach in major college football the next year. A victory over Texas A&M in the Alamo Bowl had given Paterno 316 career victories, and he needed just seven more to supplant the Bear.

Seven victories in 2000 seemed reasonable, because Paterno's Nittany Lions had won seven games or more every season since 1967 except for six wins in 1984 and five in 1988, when Penn State had its first losing season in 50 years. Yet, there was a bad omen.

The 1999 team had underachieved, losing three straight at the end of the regular season after being No. 2 in the rankings all year. Losing can be contagious, and the last time Paterno's Lions had lost three straight was in the middle of that depressing 1988 season, and they then lost two more games to close out 1988 with another defeat in the 1989 season opener.

No one really thought such a losing streak would ever happen again to Paterno, but it did in 1999, and it got worse. The 2000 team didn't lose three in a row but finished a disappointing 5–7. That left Paterno just one away from tying the Bear, but the losing continued in 2001 as Penn State lost its first four games of the season for the first time in 115 years. The Lions had never been ahead in any of the defeats, and the clamor for Paterno to retire began to intensify.

A backup redshirt freshman quarterback came to Paterno's rescue in week five. Penn State was playing its best game of the year at Northwestern, but with 1:39 left, the Lions trailed 35–31 with the ball on their own 48-yard line when 19-year-old Zack Mills entered the game to replace State's injured starting quarterback. Eight plays later, Mills threw a four-yard touchdown pass with 22 seconds remaining, and Paterno tied the Bear.

Ohio State was a seven-point favorite the next week in newly expanded Beaver Stadium where 12,000 seats, including private suites and a club section, had boosted seating capacity past 107,000. A standing-room crowd of 108,327 moaned as Ohio State took a commanding 27–9 lead less than three minutes into the second half on an interception that had bounced off the hands of the Lions' wide-open receiver.

But on the second play after the kickoff, Mills, who had not started the game, ran an option right on a play designed to pick up seven or eight yards, and he broke down the sideline for 69 yards and a touchdown. Even though a pass attempt for two points failed, Ohio State seemed stunned. A few minutes later, Shawn Mayer recovered a Buckeyes fumble near midfield, and two plays later Mills threw a 26-yard touchdown pass to Tony Johnson. When the Lions regained possession after an Ohio State punt, Mills drove the Lions 90 yards on 10 plays to take the lead for the first time, at 29–27, on a 14-yard touchdown pass to Eric McCoo with 13 seconds gone in the fourth quarter.

The Buckeyes used 10 plays in driving to the Lions' 17-yard line for a fourth-and-6 with 3:31 remaining, and Mike Nugent came on to try a 34-yard field goal.

On the snap, the left side of Penn State's defense surged forward and upward. Cornerback Bryan Scott rushed in

and jumped behind 6'5", 330-pound junior tackle Jimmy Kennedy who also was jumping, and Kennedy reached up with his beefy right hand and batted the ball away. There was 2:55 remaining, and the Lions ran out the clock.

Later Kennedy would say he had timed his first jump poorly, and it was his second jump that made it happen. "I was thinking, *Block this kick*." Kennedy said. "It just so happened, I got it. Aw, man…I got Joe No. 324."

As the jubilant crowd cheered and chanted "324" and "JoePa, JoePa," the players carried Paterno to a portable stage where his wife, five children, nine grandchildren, and several university officials waited. As tears welled up behind his trademark thick glasses, the 74-year-old

Game Details

Penn State 29 • Ohio State 27

Ohio State	7	6	14	0	27
Penn State	6	3	13	7	29

Date: October 27, 2001

Team Records: Penn State 1–4, Ohio State 4–2

Scoring Plays:

OSU—Jenkins 66-yard pass from Bellisari (Nugent PAT)
PSU—Gould 23-yard FG
PSU—Gould 46-yard FG
OSU—Nugent 28-yard FG
PSU—Gould 46-yard FG
OSU—Nugent 19-yard FG
OSU—Wells 65-yard run (Nugent PAT)
OSU—Ross 45-yard interception return (Nugent PAT)
PSU—Mills 69-yard run (pass failed)
PSU—T. Johnson 26-yard pass from Mills (Gould PAT)
PSU—McCoo 14-yard pass from Mills (Gould PAT)

Paterno and Bowden

Joe Paterno or his friend Bobby Bowden will someday be the ultimate winningest coach in major college football. They are both nearing the end of their legendary careers, and as the 2009 season began, Paterno had won 383 games—one ahead of Bowden. But Bowden could lose 10–14 victories from the 2006 and 2007 seasons because of an NCAA penalty that is still pending against the FSU athletic department for major academic infractions.

No coach in history has won more games at one school than Paterno. Because of the precariousness of the profession, it's unlikely anyone will ever break that Paterno record. And with all the vagaries built into modern-day football and the pressure on coaches, the final mark of either Paterno or Bowden will probably stand forever.

However, Penn State fans believe Bowden's win total is inflated by a puzzling 1978 NCAA ruling. Bowden's first 31 victories from 1959 to 1962 were at his alma mater Howard, a small school in Birmingham now known as Samford. Included among Bowden's conquests were Millsaps, Southwest Lynx, and Mississippi Delta. When the NCAA created separate categories for small and major colleges, it ruled that when a coach in any sport had spent 10 years at a major college, all of his or her victories at any four-

Joe Paterno and Bobby Bowden, the two winningest coaches in history, shake hands after the 2006 Orange Bowl. *Photo courtesy of Steve Manuel*

year school count on his or her all-time listing.

As Pittsburgh sportswriter Bob Smizik wrote, that's like officially counting all the home runs hit in the minor leagues in the home-run totals for baseball players who play more than 10 years in the major leagues.

With Paterno, 82, and Bowden, 79, still going strong, the competition continues.

Paterno told the crowd, "I can't put into words how I really feel about this football team, this university, and you fans. I'm really overwhelmed and just emotionally drained. You never think it's going to be a big deal until it happens."

But the season that started at the time the country was attacked on September 11 ended with another losing year, and it would be five more years before Paterno could turn his program around. By that time, the Bear and 324 were history, and Paterno had Florida State's Bobby Bowden as competition for the all-time coaching record.

> **I**t's just overwhelming; it'll take me a long time to realize. I am overwhelmed right now. I am struggling here to not say something that sounds stupid; I usually do that when we lose. I was amazed with the emotion the squad showed, so I am glad it's over.
>
> **—JOE PATERNO**

November 10, 1979

Herbie's Miracle Field Goal

Herb Menhardt's 54-yard Field Goal on Last Play Saves Season

Of all the field goals that have won games for Penn State, Herb Menhardt's 54-yard boot with one second on the clock that beat North Carolina State 9–7 in 1979 was the most thrilling and electrifying.

Minutes after the dynamic kick before a stunned capacity NC State crowd of 51,200, coach Joe Paterno told his junior place-kicker, "Herbie, in all the years I've been coaching—30 years—that's the greatest football play I've ever seen."

Menhardt's field goal is still just one yard short of the Penn State school record, set by Chris Bahr, who kicked three for 55 yards during the 1975 season.

The kick and the victory salvaged what was a disappointing season but one that would have been much worse without the last-minute heroics of Menhardt and the Nittany Lions offense. Expectations had been high that year, following 1978 when Penn State became No. 1 for the first time ever. But off-the-field problems, a leadership vacuum, an erratic offense, and a rash of injuries sent the team into disarray. A preseason No. 5 ranking turned to mush as the Lions were soundly beaten by Texas A&M,

Nebraska, and underdog Miami before traveling to Raleigh with a 5–3 record.

The game was rated a toss-up. NC State sported a 6–3 record behind a potent running attack and a solid defense, but Penn State was hurting, using a patched-up defense without several injured starters, including All-American linemen Bruce Clark and Matt Millen. It was a defensive struggle almost to the end with Menhardt field goals of 38 and 37 yards giving the Lions a close 6–0 lead until late in the fourth quarter when the Wolfpack offense came alive and drove 72 yards on 14 plays to take the lead with just 1:18 left in the game.

Freshman Curt Warner returned the NC State kickoff to the Lions' 24-yard line, and three quick plays later a 15-yard pass from Dayle Tate to tight end Brad Scovill put the ball on the PSU 41. On second down Tate was sacked for a 14-yard loss, and an incomplete pass left the Lions with a fourth-and-24 with 24 seconds and one timeout remaining. The crowd was delirious.

With a four-receiver set sprinting downfield, Tate scrambled to avoid the rush and found split end Terry Rakowsky wide open near the Wolfpack 40-yard line. Until a month before, Rakowsky had been the Lions' backup quarterback. He leaped between two defenders to make the first catch of his career and picked up a first down at the NC State 37. Tate quickly lined up the team and threw the ball out of bounds with seven seconds left.

Surprisingly, Paterno called for a pass—to gain a few more yards before the field-goal attempt, he said later—

and it almost cost the Lions the game. But the pass was incomplete. One second remained.

Menhardt's longest field goal had been 47 yards in high school, and this was the junior's first season as the Lions' kicker. His regular holder was injured, so starting tailback Mike Guman was now the holder at the left hash mark. "Let's hit it, Herb," Guman said.

Dayle Tate's (right) pass to Terry Rakowsky (left) set up the miracle field goal that won the game for Penn State.
Photos courtesy of the Penn State Pattee-Paterno Library Sports Archives

Herb Menhardt's 54-yard field goal on the last play of the game saved the day for Penn State. *Photo courtesy of Penn State Athletic Communications*

Herb Menhardt

Herb Menhardt is almost forgotten today. What he did 30 years ago is but a fading memory compared to the more recent accomplishments of such kickers as Craig Fayak, Brett Conway, and Kevin Kelly.

But the Flourtown, Pennsylvania, native still holds one of the most difficult of all Penn State kicking records—extra-point accuracy in a career. He never missed an extra point in 54 attempts in the two seasons he kicked, 1979 and 1980.

It is a field goal Menhardt missed as a non-lettering freshman in 1976 that made him so good later. Penn State was trailing Iowa 7–6 but with less than a minute remaining with a fourth-and-goal at the Hawkeyes' 8-yard line.

On a hunch, Paterno sent in Menhardt instead of sophomore starting kicker Matt Bahr. The angle on the right hash mark was difficult, the center snap was low, and the holder had difficulty getting the ball set. Menhardt shanked the ball wide left and has said his failure that day led him to study "performance enhancement and stress management" to help him on the field.

Menhardt also was a standout on Penn State's varsity soccer team, and in 1977 and 1978 he concentrated on soccer and didn't even practice with the football team in 1978.

But it all paid off in the next two years. In addition to his historic kick at North Carolina State, Menhardt's 14 field goals (on 20 attempts) in 1979 and his 15 (on 21 attempts) in 1980 remain among the top 10 in the Penn State record book for number of field goals scored in a season.

"When I hit it, I knew it was in the area," Menhardt said after the game. "It was a question of whether it would hit the post and bounce back or go in." The ball skimmed off the inside right post and over the crossbar.

"This was one of the greatest wins for Penn State," Paterno said at the time.

The Nittany Lions would go on to finish with an 8–4 record, a 9–6 win over Tulane in the Liberty Bowl, and a No. 20 ranking by the Associated Press. Herbie made it happen.

> The way he walked out on the field, you knew he could make it.... This was a very emotional game for both teams. It was the kind of game where you don't like to see either team lose.
>
> —JOE PATERNO

Game Details

Penn State 9 • North Carolina State 7

Penn State	3	0	3	3	**9**
NC State	0	0	0	7	**7**

Date: November 10, 1979
Team Records: Penn State 5–3, North Carolina State 6–3

Scoring Plays:
PSU—Menhardt 38-yard FG
PSU—Menhardt 37-yard FG
NCS—Smith two-yard run (Ritter PAT)
PSU—Menhardt 54-yard FG

The **Picks**

Pete Giftopoulos intercepts Vinny Testaverde at the goal line on the last play of the game to defeat Miami and win the national championship on January 2, 1987. *Photo courtesy of the Penn State All-Sports Museum*

January 2, 1987

The Last Interception

Pete Giftopoulos Intercepts Vinny Testaverde at Goal Line on Last Play to Win National Championship

Linebacker Pete Giftopoulos didn't just happen to be in the right place at the right time when he made the last-second goal-line interception in the Fiesta Bowl that gave Penn State its second national championship. The 1986 defense had an unwritten motto that was at the heart of their unity and teamwork on the field, and they often shouted it at each other during the heated, tense moments of a game: "Someone make the play."

And in 1986 there always was that someone there to make the play. With the return of 19 of the best 22 offensive players and 18 of the best defensive players from the 1985 team that lost the championship to Oklahoma in the Orange Bowl, the Nittany Lions were in everyone's preseason top 10.

But the offense had been erratic throughout the season, and the defense made most of the big plays to win the games. When the No. 6–ranked Lions shot to No. 2 with a decisive 23–3 upset at then–No. 2 Alabama in the seventh game of the season, the defense intercepted two passes, had five sacks, recovered three of five forced fumbles, and held Alabama's running game to 44 yards on 33 carries.

Miami had been at the top of the polls most of the year. Quarterback Vinny Testaverde won the Heisman Trophy directing a balanced offense that averaged 38 points a game while the defense limited opponents to less than 13 points per game. The Hurricanes were a six-and-a-half-point favorite, but their boorish behavior during game week turned the media and the Arizona populous against them, and during the pregame warm-ups they taunted the Lions players. But Penn State set the tone of the game early by intimidating the talented Miami receivers with crunching hits that made them miss or drop passes.

Testaverde had completed nearly 64 percent of his 276 pass attempts for 26 touchdowns with just nine interceptions. But State's defensive coordinator Jerry Sandusky designed a new technique to confuse Testaverde by foregoing the blitz and dropping eight players into the passing zones.

With the defensive scheme working to perfection and the punting of John Bruno keeping Miami far away from the Penn State goal for most of the game, the teams slugged their way through three quarters to a 7–7 draw. Miami scored first after recovering a Lions fumble at the PSU 23-yard line early in the second quarter, and State responded with a 74-yard, 13-play drive to tie it.

Both teams missed field goals in the second half until a 38-yard field goal with 11:49 left in the fourth quarter gave Miami the lead. The Hurricanes immediately forced a punt, but All-American linebacker Shane Conlan then made the second-biggest play of the game. He intercepted

his second Testaverde pass of the half at the Miami 44-yard line, and, despite a sore left knee and right ankle, Conlan somehow hobbled his way to the 5. Two plays later, the Lions led 14–10 with 8:13 remaining.

After the kickoff, Trey Bauer caused a fumble, but State's offense sputtered. The two teams traded punts until Bruno's ninth punt of the game gave Miami the ball at its own 23-yard line with 3:07 on the clock and all three timeouts left. Three plays yielded just four yards, but on a fourth-and-6 at its own 27 with 2:24 on the clock, Miami coach Jimmy Johnson gambled. Testaverde hit Brian Blades on a quick out near the left sideline, and he ran to the PSU 41.

It was the spark Miami needed, and Joe Paterno admitted later he was worried. "In my experience, whenever I've taken a big, big gamble like that and made it, I've usually won," he said. In four quick passes, the Hurricanes had a first down at the Penn State 9 with 1:01 left.

With the 73,098 screaming fans on their feet, Testaverde found Michael Irvin for four yards. On second down he had Irvin open for a touchdown across the middle, but he was sacked by tackle Tim Johnson,

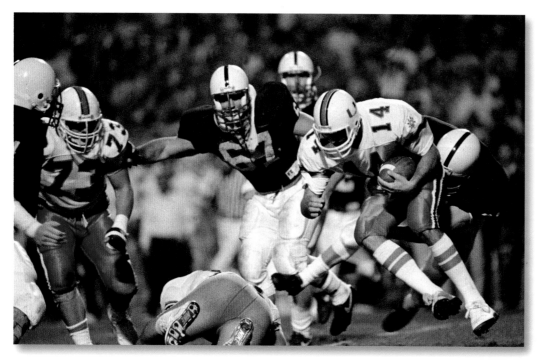

Pete Giftopoulos, behind right, slams into Miami quarterback Vinny Testaverde (No. 14) for a sack in the third quarter of the Fiesta Bowl in Tempe, Arizona, on January 2, 1987. *Photo courtesy of AP Images*

John Bruno

Punter John Bruno was the unsung star of the 1987 Fiesta Bowl, both on the field and off it.

If not for his outstanding punting that kept Miami continually digging out from poor field position, the flow of the game—and the outcome—might have been different. Bruno kicked nine punts for a game average of 43.4 yards per kick, and three of the boots were downed inside the Miami 2-, 9-, and 11-yard lines.

Yet he is best known by Penn State fans for something that happened at a pregame steak fry for both teams. The cocky Miami players were there dressed in army fatigues, and early in the evening they shocked the rest of the guests by storming out after one Miami player shouted, "The Japanese [didn't] go and have dinner with Pearl Harbor before they bombed them."

But as the stunned audience watched, Bruno grabbed the microphone and said, "Excuse me, but didn't the Japanese lose the war?" The crowd cheered and applauded, and the incident turned the Penn State team into hometown folk heroes. "Class Beats Crass," read the headline in the *Phoenix Gazette* after Penn State won the game.

What most people didn't know at the time was that Bruno had fought skin cancer two years earlier and it was in remission. Unfortunately, the cancer returned in December 1991, and John Bruno passed away on April 13, 1992.

and Miami called timeout with 25 seconds remaining. On third down Testaverde missed halfback Warren Williams. Testaverde went to the line with 18 seconds left. "Somebody's got to make a play," Conlan yelled as the Miami coaches feverishly tried to get their quarterback to call a timeout.

Three receivers sped out, but Testaverde looked solely at Brett Perriman in the left corner of the end zone and threw. Four Lions defenders converged on Perriman. Giftopoulos swept in front of Perriman at the goal line and ran to the 10 before he fell on his knees clutching the ball firmly.

Once again "someone" had a made a play, only this one was for the national championship.

> **W**e dropped eight people, and the three on line did a great job of getting pressure. Teams have a tendency to run a quick post near the goal, and I didn't have to move. He threw it right at me.
>
> —PETE GIFTOPOULOS

Game Details

Penn State 14 • Miami 10

Miami	0	7	0	3	**10**
Penn State	0	7	0	7	**14**

Date: January 2, 1987

Team Records: Penn State 11–0, Miami 11–0

Scoring Plays:

MIA—Bratton one-yard run (Cox PAT)

PSU—Shaffer four-yard run (Manca PAT)

MIA—Seelig 38-yard FG

PSU—Dozier six-yard run (Manca PAT)

September 7, 1985

Zordich Sets the Tone in the Heat

Interception on Second Play of Season Starts Lions on Way to National Championship Game

In Penn State's illustrious football history, no play was as unique and as consequential as Michael Zordich's dramatic interception in the first game of the 1985 season at Maryland. The circumstances were most unusual, with blistering heat on the field and Maryland hyped as a preseason contender for the national championship versus a lightly regarded Penn State team coming off a ragtag 6–5 season. Zordich's 32-yard return for a touchdown changed everything—the spontaneous catalyst for a surprising undefeated regular season that would take the Nittany Lions to No. 1 in the polls and land them in the national championship game in the Orange Bowl.

The 1984 season had been the worst since coach Joe Paterno's first year as head coach in 1966. And with two humiliating losses at the end—44–7 to Notre Dame and 31–11 to Pitt—the Nittany Lions missed out on a postseason bowl game for the first time in 14 years. Some improvement was expected in 1985, but with a roster loaded with redshirt juniors, Penn State was hardly mentioned in anyone's top 10 teams and was ranked No. 19 in the preseason AP poll. Maryland was in almost everyone's top 10, and *Sport Magazine* had picked the Terps as No. 1.

What's more, Penn State had lost only once to Maryland in 28 previous games. The raucous and mostly partisan Terps crowd of 50,750 that poured into Byrd Stadium in the sweltering heat on September 7, 1985, was confident that this was their day of atonement.

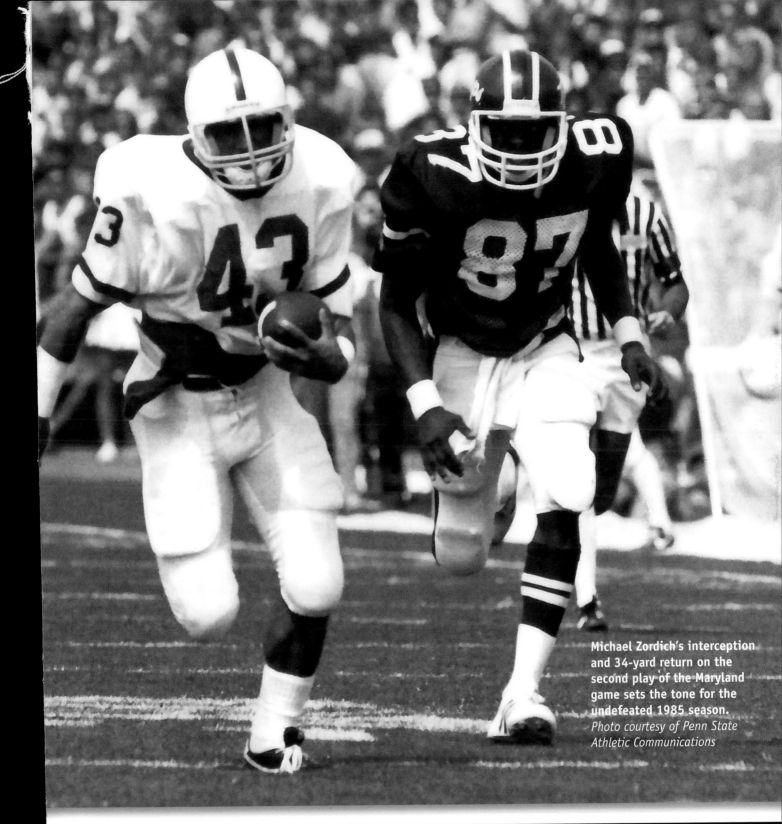

Michael Zordich's interception and 34-yard return on the second play of the Maryland game sets the tone for the undefeated 1985 season.
Photo courtesy of Penn State Athletic Communications

There has never been a hotter game on record for Penn State. Temperatures reached 120 degrees on the field with humidity of at least 80 percent. Despite electric cooling fans and liquids on the sideline, several players from both teams threw up. Penn State won the coin toss and surprised the fans by kicking off, but Paterno had his reason.

Paterno and his coaching staff had reassessed his entire team since the end of 1984. He and defensive coordinator Jerry Sandusky had tinkered with the Lions' defense and came up with an adjusted 4-4-3 that was more like a 5-2-4 stacked defense. They believed defense was now the team's strength and that it could cope with Maryland's ball-control offense.

"We were using a lot of odd fronts, stacking linebackers," Sandusky said. "We went to a seven-man front, as opposed to an eight-man front, and a four-deep secondary. But there was a lot of uncertainty going into the Maryland game about how far our defense had come."

Maryland ran the kickoff back to the 25-yard line and, on the first play from scrimmage, sent its running back into the line for a short gain just to feel out the Lions' defense. Now it was coach Bobby Ross' turn to test State's new defensive alignment. He called for a quick screen pass to Maryland's star receiver, Azizuddin Abdur-Ra'oof in the right flat. Veteran quarterback Stan Gelbaugh took the snap, dropped back one step, and fired.

Zordich, Penn State's strong safety and a senior co-captain, remembered what happened next. "I remember the defensive call," said Zordich. "It was three-jack [or three-deep zone coverage], and I stepped in front of the ball and there was no one between me and the end zone. When I planted my feet, my shoe came off and I took off. I remembered how fast the receiver was, and I didn't want him to catch me."

It had been 50 seconds since the kickoff, and the game was nowhere near over. The Lions continued to stymie the demoralized Terps and built up a 17–0 lead early in the

Massimo Manca's two field goals and two extra points made the difference in Penn State's 20–18 upset of Maryland. *Photo courtesy of Penn State Athletic Communications*

Michael Zordich

Michael Zordich didn't have the pure athletic ability of some of his Penn State teammates, but there was nobody on the field who was tougher or more physical.

Losing the 1985 national championship game to Oklahoma in the Orange Bowl still rankles him. "That one hurt quite a bit," Zordich said. "When I reflect I still get a little pain in my stomach about it."

Despite his collegiate success, the NFL didn't think much of Zordich's chances. He wasn't drafted until the ninth round by the San Diego Chargers and then was quickly cut. Even though others doubted, he was determined to play in the NFL, and the next season he was on the special teams of the New York Jets. Two years later he was starting for the Phoenix Cardinals

and eventually spent five years with Phoenix and another five years with Philadelphia before retiring.

"I worked extremely hard to stay in the NFL for 12 years," Zordich said, "and what I learned from Joe Paterno was a big part of that. Joe would always say keep your poise, things don't always go as you plan, and with hard work and time things will work out."

second quarter. By halftime Maryland was back in the game, 17–10, after recovering a fumbled Penn State kickoff return. Midway through the third quarter the Terps jumped into the lead for the first time, with an interception inside the Lions' 40-yard line that set up a quick touchdown and a surprising pass for two extra points by kick-holder Dan Henning. But 90 seconds later Penn State regained the lead for good, 20–18, on a 46-yard field goal by Massimo Manca.

Maryland threatened several times as time wound down, missing field goals from 34 and 51 yards. Then with 1:24 left, Maryland drove from its own 24 to the Penn State 33, and Gelbaugh hit Alvin Blount on a short pass with about 38 seconds left. Cornerback Lance Hamilton stripped the ball, linebacker Trey Bauer recovered, and the game was over.

Maryland had controlled the ball for 36 minutes and had run off 83 plays for 342 net yards while State had just 59 plays for 249 yards. But it was one of those 83 Maryland plays that made the biggest difference of all—not just for that game but for the entire 1985 season.

Game Details

Penn State 20 • Maryland 18

Penn State	10	7	3	0	**20**
Maryland	0	10	8	0	**18**

Date: September 7, 1985

Team Records: Penn State 0–0, Maryland 0–0

Scoring Plays:

PSU—Zordich 32-yard interception (Manca PAT)

PSU—Manca 28-yard FG

PSU—Williams two-yard pass from Shaffer (Manca PAT)

MD—Paredes 22-yard FG

MD—Badanjek eight-yard run (Paredes PAT)

MD—Badanjek five-yard run (Knight pass from Henning PAT)

PSU—Manca 46-yard FG

November 28, 1981

The Great Hurricane in Pitt Stadium

Lions Come from Behind on Second-Quarter Interceptions and Rout No. 1 Pitt 48–14

Until Penn State entered the Big Ten in 1993, the Nittany Lions' most embittered rivalry was with the University of Pittsburgh, tracing its rancorous roots to the first game in 1893. The acrimony has waned since 2001, when the teams stopped playing almost annually, but whenever longtime State fans are asked to recall their most satisfying Lions victory of all time, the shocking 48–14 victory at Pitt Stadium in 1981 is up there with the two national championship bowl games.

It isn't just because Pitt was the No. 1 team in the nation at the time and the win was so decisive. What really made the victory so gratifying—and one the Nittany Lions nation will gloat about forever—were the intriguing circumstances leading up to the game and the bizarre way everything played out on the field.

Both teams had been rated in the preseason top 10, and after the fifth game of the season, Penn State had climbed to No. 1 in the AP poll with Pitt just six measly votes behind at No. 2. But two weeks later, the Lions were

upset at Beaver Stadium by Miami and then lost again at home to Alabama. By the time of the Pitt game on the Saturday after Thanksgiving, Pitt was No. 1 and set for a national championship game against No. 3 Georgia in the Sugar Bowl, while the reeling No. 11 Lions had agreed to play No. 8 USC in the first Fiesta Bowl that would be played on New Year's Day.

With State's schedule rated the second toughest in the nation, a sarcastic verbal warfare broke out when senior linebacker Chet Parlavecchio mocked Pitt's schedule. "Our schedule was like going through a hurricane, and Pitt's schedule was like going through a Bermuda sun shower," the New Jersey linebacker grumbled. Pitt coach Jackie Sherrill, who was already feuding with State's Joe Paterno over some off-field incidents, said Parlavecchio didn't have the class to get into Pitt. Early in the second quarter with the game still in doubt, the two almost had a fistfight when Parlavecchio was penalized for a late hit on Pitt receiver Dwight Collins in front of the Pitt bench.

Pitt was favored by just a touchdown, and the Panthers came out of the locker room to rub some Lions' noses into

Mark Robinson made one of the two plays that turned around the Penn State–Pitt game on November 28, 1981. *Photo courtesy of the Penn State Pattee-Paterno Library Sports Archives*

Todd Blackledge scores the second touchdown against Pitt on November 28, 1981.
Photo courtesy of Penn State Athletic Communications

looked deep in the end zone for Collins, who had caught his first two touchdown passes, but safety Roger Jackson leaped up and grabbed the ball. It would be the turning-point play of the game, but no one realized it at the time.

In three minutes, the Lions went 80 yards on eight plays for a touchdown primarily on the passing of redshirt sophomore quarterback Todd Blackledge. But moments later, with the help of the 15-yard penalty on Parlavecchio, Pitt was banging away again with a third-and-3 at the PSU 28-yard line when Marino drilled a pass to Julius Dawkins crossing at the 2-yard line in what would be the second defining play of the game. Jackson belted Dawkins so hard they fell to the ground momentarily stunned and didn't see the ball pop up. Lions sophomore safety Mark Robinson grabbed it at the goal line and ran 17 yards before being tackled.

This time Pitt held, but the throw to Dawkins would be the Panthers' last serious threat. With less than three minutes left in the half, a 52-yard pass to Roger Jackson's brother, All-American junior receiver Kenny Jackson, set up an eight-yard touchdown by Blackledge capping a quick six-play, 80-yard drive.

Six minutes into the second half the game was all but over. On the fourth play of the third quarter, Roger Jackson forced a fumble that Parlavecchio recovered at State's 44-yard line, and Kenny Jackson scored on a 42-yard pass from Blackledge. Less than three minutes later, Blackledge and Jackson hooked up on a 45-yard pass that made the score 28–14. The rout was on, but the humiliation of Pitt wasn't. The Lions scored again early in the fourth quarter, and with less than six minutes remaining, Robinson put the final knife into Marino and the Panthers by running

the ground—and they did. Pitt's defense completely shut down State's multiple offense in the first quarter, holding it to minus-1 yard as junior quarterback Dan Marino, leading the nation with 34 touchdown passes, threw for two touchdowns as he took the Panthers on dominating drives of 53 and 64 yards. When the quarter came to a close, Marino had completed nine of 10 passes, and he had Pitt poised to turn the game into a rout with a second-and-7 at State's 31-yard line.

Marino took the first snap of the second quarter, and that's when the great hurricane hit the Panthers. Marino

91 yards on another interception—with only one shoe, no less—for the last State touchdown.

Chet Parlavecchio's Great Hurricane had just devastated Pitt Stadium, and the headline in the *New York Times* said it all: "Penn State Routs No. 1 Pitt, 48–14." And to make it all even more satisfying, this was Pitt coach Jackie Sherrill's 38th birthday!

> **I** thought we were going to have a war. I didn't try to hurt [Pitt receiver Dwight Collins] or anything. I think we needed something to give us a spark.
>
> —CHET PARLAVECCHIO

Game Details

Penn State 48 • Pitt 14

Penn State	0	14	17	17	**48**
Pitt	14	0	0	0	**14**

Date: November 28, 1981
Team Records: Penn State 8–2, Pitt 10–0

Scoring Plays:

PITT—Collins 28-yard pass from Marino (Everett PAT)
PITT—Collins nine-yard pass from Marino (Everett PAT)
PSU—Meade two-yard run (Franco PAT)
PSU—Blackledge eight-yard run (Franco PAT)
PSU—K. Jackson 42-yard pass from Blackledge (Franco PAT)
PSU—K. Jackson 45-yard pass from Blackledge (Franco PAT)
PSU—Franco 39-yard FG
PSU—Franco 38-yard FG
PSU—Farrell recovered fumble in end zone (Franco PAT)
PSU—Robinson 91-yard interception return (Franco PAT)

Penn State vs. Pitt

Penn State's rivalry with Pittsburgh once had the intensity and animosity that was on par with the other great college football season-ending games such as Michigan–Ohio State, Army–Navy, and Alabama–Auburn. In the almost annual 96 games since the first one in 1893, there have been dozens where one team spoiled the other's entire season with an upset. Two of the biggest upsets were in 1940 and 1948, when Pitt ruined State's unbeaten seasons and New Year's Day bowl opportunities. Penn State did the same thing to Pitt in 1952.

And Penn State fans will never forget the 1981 game when the No. 11 Lions shocked the No. 1 Panthers 48–14 before their own fans at Pitt Stadium, knocking them out of the national championship race.

Until Joe Paterno became State's head coach in 1966, most of the games were played in Pittsburgh. Over the decades Penn State fans had grown tired and embittered by the atmosphere surrounding the game in Pittsburgh. Paterno's winning teams and the increasing capacity of Beaver Stadium changed all that.

Since the series ended in 2000, Pitt has sought future games, but Penn State has insisted that two of every three games be played at Beaver Stadium for financial reasons, and Pitt has declined. Penn State is now ahead in the series, with 50 wins, 42 losses, and four ties. Just 23 of those games have been played at Penn State with 66 in Pittsburgh. Somehow, that just doesn't seem fair, but after all it is a rivalry—or was once.

25 Other Great Plays

From 1887 Through 2008 (In Chronological Order)

October 20, 1906, at New Haven—PS 0, Yale 10: Mother Dunn blocks punt but Cy Cyphers, picks it up, and runs wrong way as State outplays defending national champions.

October 28, 1911, at Philadelphia—PS 22, Pennsylvania 7: Shorty Miller's scintillating 95-yard opening kickoff return sparks first victory over then–No.1 rival Penn.

November 16, 1912, at Columbus—PS 1, Ohio State 0 (PS 37–0): Ohio State walks off field (and forfeits) with seven minutes left after Dex Very's vicious block on kickoff return.

November 27, 1919, at Pittsburgh—PS 20, Pitt 0: Bob Higgins sets record that still stands with 92-yard touchdown reception off fake punt in last win over Pitt for 20 years.

October 22, 1921, at Cambridge—PS 21, Harvard 21: Substitute Harry Wilson runs 60 yards to set up Lions touchdown, but favored Harvard scores in near darkness to salvage tie.

October 29, 1921, at NY Polo Grounds—PS 28, Georgia Tech 7: Glenn Killinger's 85-yard touchdown on opening kickoff shocks favored Tech and makes Killinger an All-American.

October 20, 1923, at Beaver Field—PS 21, Navy 3: Light Horse Harry Wilson scores touchdowns on 55-yard interception, 95-yard kickoff return, and 72-yard run in greatest PSU one-man performance.

October 26, 1929, at Beaver Field—PS 6, Lafayette 3: Cooper French and Frank Diedrich team up for a dramatic 60-yard lateral punt-return touchdown on last play of game.

November 25, 1939, at Beaver Field—PS 10, Pitt 0: Leon Gajecki and Carl Stravinski force fumble that Gajecki recovers, and Lions beat Pitt for first time in 20 years.

January 1, 1948, at Dallas (Cotton Bowl)—PS 13, Southern Methodist 13: Ed Czekaj and Doak Walker miss extra-point kicks, and State drops pass in the end zone on last play of milestone game.

October 17, 1953, at Beaver Field—PS 20, Syracuse 14: Danny DeFalco's blocked punt helps win game late in fourth quarter as Lenny Moore's interception ignites brawl on Syracuse sideline.

September 25, 1954, at Champaign, IL—PS 14, Illinois 12: Beatle Bailey and Lenny Moore combine for run-lateral touchdown in major upset that shocks college football.

November 7, 1964, at Columbus—PS 27, Ohio State 0: Glenn Ressler's blocking and defensive play leads 3–4 Nittany Lions to stunning upset over No. 2 Ohio State.

November 10, 1973, at Beaver Stadium—PS 35, North Carolina State 29: John Cappelletti sets school record of 41 carries in rushing for 231 yards and three touchdowns.

November 22, 1975, at Three Rivers Stadium—PSU 7, Pitt 6: Lions block extra point and Pitt kicker misses two field goals late in fourth quarter to avoid embarrassing loss.

November 26, 1977, at Pittsburgh—PS 15, Pitt 13: End-zone interceptions by Ron Hostettler and Matt Millen's tackle on two-point conversion on last play save 11–1 season.

November 4, 1978, at Beaver Stadium—Penn State 27, Maryland 3: Five interceptions and five sacks help win "Battle of Unbeatens" that helps propel Lions toward national championship game.

October 12, 1985, at Beaver Stadium—PS 19, Alabama 17: Lions rally in fourth quarter on Michael Timpson reverse and two-yard touchdown pass from Matt Knizer to Brian Siverling to remain undefeated.

October 11, 1986, at Beaver Stadium—PS 23, Cincinnati 17: Tackle by Pete Curkendall and reception by sophomore reserve Blair Thomas brings favored Lions from behind to stay unbeaten.

October 25, 1986, at Tuscaloosa—PS 23, Alabama 3: No. 6 Lions upsets No. 2 Alabama as defense intercepts two passes and recovers three fumbles to set up touchdown and two field goals.

November 8, 1986, at Beaver Stadium—PS 17, MD 15: Duffy Cobbs knocks down pass for two-point conversion at 1-yard line on last play of game to stay in contention for national title.

November 21, 1987, at Beaver Stadium—PS 21, Notre Dame 20: Pete Curkendall tackles Tony Rice's attempt for two points in last second to destroy Irish national championship chances.

January 1, 1992, at Tempe, AZ (Fiesta Bowl)—PS 42, Tennessee 17: Lions come from behind with 35 points in less than eight minutes to clinch 8–2 season and No. 3 ranking.

October 29, 1994, at Beaver Stadium—PS 63, Ohio State 14: Kerry Collins passes for two touchdowns, and Ki-Jana Carter scores four touchdowns as Lions overwhelm Buckeyes but still lose No. 1 AP ranking.

January 3, 2005, at Orange Bowl—PS 26, FSU 21: Ethan Kilmer's leaping touchdown reception in end zone with five seconds left in first half enables Kevin Kelly to kick winning field goal in third overtime.